W9-AOY-136

Fix-It and Forget-It® SLOW COOKER FREEZER MEALS

150 MAKE-AHEAD MEALS TO SAVE YOU TIME AND MONEY

HOPE COMERFORD

Photos by Bonnie Matthews

Good Books

New York, New York

Copyright © 2018 by Good Books, an imprint of Skyhorse Publishing, Inc.

Photos by Bonnie Matthews

All rights reserved. No part of this book may be reproduced in any manner without the express written consent of the publisher, except in the case of brief excerpts in critical reviews or articles. All inquiries should be addressed to Good Books, 307 West 36th Street, 11th Floor, New York, NY 10018.

Good Books books may be purchased in bulk at special discounts for sales promotion, corporate gifts, fund-raising, or educational purposes. Special editions can also be created to specifications. For details, contact the Special Sales Department, Good Books, 307 West 36th Street, 11th Floor, New York, NY 10018 or info@skyhorsepublishing.com.

Good Books is an imprint of Skyhorse Publishing, Inc.®, a Delaware corporation.

Visit our website at www.goodbooks.com.

10 9 8 7 6 5 4 3 2 1

Library of Congress Cataloging-in-Publication Data is available on file.

Cover design by Mona Lin
Cover photo by Bonnie Matthews

Print ISBN: 978-1-68099-390-5
Ebook ISBN: 978-1-68099-392-9

Printed in China

Table of Contents

Welcome to Fix-It and Forget-It Freezer Meals ⚘ 1

How Does This Book Work? ⚘ 1

A Guide to Freezer Meals ⚘ 2

Freezing Tips ⚘ 4

Choosing a Slow Cooker ⚘ 4

Slow Cooking Tips and Tricks and Other Things You May Not Know ⚘ 7

Breakfast ⚘ 11

Chicken & Turkey Main Dishes ⚘ 29

Beef Main Dishes ⚘ 91

Pork Main Dishes ⚘ 151

Meatless & Seafood Main Dishes ⚘ 223

Soups, Stews & Chilis ⚘ 259

Metric Equivalent Measurements ⚘ 330

Recipe and Ingredient Index ⚘ 331

About the Author ⚘ 343

Welcome to Fix-It and Forget-It Freezer Meals

About four years ago, I ordered a freezer meal workshop kit. My hope was to have some meals ready to go when life got hectic. I took the time one weekend to assemble all ten meals in the kit, then stuck them in my freezer to cook at a later date. It took me a couple hours that day to assemble them, but I was left with ten assembled meals I could pull out of the freezer whenever I needed and cook when I was ready! I LOVED how convenient it was! All that prep work, done at once, was a not so bad. I've attended several other freezer meal workshops since and always assemble at least twenty meals to keep in my freezer for our super busy times of the year.

This got me thinking . . . why not put together my own freezer meal cookbook?! So, I did! In this book, you'll find 150 freezer meal recipes that you can prepare ahead of time in freezer bags and then pull out of the freezer when you're ready to cook them. Sometimes everything you'll need will be right in the bag. Sometimes you'll need a few other ingredients at cooking time (i.e. milk, rice or quinoa, sour cream, etc.), but that will be noted for you in the recipe instructions.

I generally pull out two or three freezer meals each week to cook. You may have a larger family, so you might pull out four to seven meals. Do what works best for your family.

This book is designed for just about anyone! Whether you're busy, you like to plan ahead, or just like things ready to go! So, let's get preppin' and pack that freezer full of goodness!

How Does This Book Work?

Each recipe is laid out in a specific fashion. First of all, you're given a glance at how many the recipe will serve, how long it will take you to prep the ingredients, and what size slow cooker would be best for the recipe. Following that, you'll have the following format:

Ingredients Needed at Time of Preparation: These are the ingredients that will go into the freezer bag.

Preparation Instructions: These are the instructions you'll need to assemble the ingredients in the bag. You'll notice that the preparation instructions will always tell you to remove as much air from the freezer bag as possible before sealing. There is more information on this in the next section, so keep reading.

Information for Freezer Bag: Everything below this heading will be what will occur when you are ready to cook your freezer meal, and will be the information needed on your bag if you so choose. I suggest printing off the label by visiting http://x.co/FIFILabel, or scanning the QR code next to the recipe. Your other options are to handwrite the instructions on the bag with a permanent marker, or to just write the title of the recipe and page number on the bag with permanent marker so you can refer back to this book once the contents of your bag have thawed. Having this information affixed to the bag is incredibly convenient, so I strongly suggest the first option.

Needed at Time of Cooking/Serving: These are the additional ingredients you'll need to either quickly finish preparing the recipe, use later in the recipe, or items you'll need at the time of serving.

Serving Suggestion: Sometimes it's nice to have some suggestions on how to serve what you're cooking. You'll find these throughout the book.

Instructions: These are the cooking instructions for when you're ready to cook your freezer meal. Notice that every recipe will instruct you to thaw the bag completely before cooking. Always thaw in a refrigerator, or in another safe manner.

Tip: Occasionally you will run across a tip that will make the recipe easier, or change it up a bit. We hope you find them helpful!

A Guide to Freezer Meals

1. Set aside an afternoon or morning to make 10–20 meals at a time. Even though it sounds like a daunting task, this book will make the process a cinch. Make a list of the recipes you want to make, then get excited! You may even consider making multiple batches of certain meals. This is going to make your life easier in the long run!

2. Make a shopping list for the recipes you're going to make. Look at all the ingredient lists for the recipes you've chosen. As you write them down, categorize your list to make shopping a breeze! I love that I can grab all the ingredients I need quickly when I'm preparing freezer meals because all of my produce, meats, seasonings,

etc. are grouped together on the list. Be sure to check in your pantry to see what you already have so you don't buy more than you need.

3. Buy precut veggies if you can. This will cut down on some of your prep time, but probably won't save you money. I like to buy precut mushrooms because I know they take a lot of prep work and I can easily find them presliced.

4. If you can't buy or find precut veggies, save some time by using your food processor. This makes chopping all the onions SO much easier!

5. Have a butcher prepare your meat for you. Just call ahead and let them know exactly what and how much you need. They may even give you a discount, all while preparing your meats just the way you need them.

6. Have lots of freezer bags on hand. You will need gallon-sized storage bags for the most part for this book. I buy them in bulk so I always have plenty on hand. If you're not a freezer bag user, then use good freezer-safe containers.

7. Make sure to label all of your freezer bags well. Always put the date you've prepared the bag on them so you know how long it's been in the freezer.

8. Print off the instructions by visiting http://x.co/FIFILabel for each recipe and affix them to the bags. This will save you a lot of time and energy! We have also conveniently included QR codes so you can scan and print off the instructions individually that way as well.

9. Be sure to thaw your freezer meals completely before cooking unless it's otherwise noted in the instructions. You will need 24 hours or more in your refrigerator to defrost them.

10. Help to avoid freezer burn by removing as much of the air as you can from your freezer bags. Little coffee stirrer straws can help you get most of the air out. Insert the straw in the center of the bag's opening (being careful not to touch the raw ingredients) and while you're sucking the air out, close the bag tightly around it, then slide the straw out and finish sealing. If you have a vacuum sealer, you may even consider that route.

11. For best results, use your freezer meals up within 4–6 months of freezing.

12. What if you want to make the meal now and freeze it later? I've included some freezing tips just in case for you in the next section.

Freezing Tips

So, what if you want to make these meals and *then* freeze them? Honestly, it's easy! You cook them, cool them, then freeze them!

Here are my tips:

1. Always let food cool completely to room temperature; cool in the refrigerator and then freeze.
2. Be sure your food is in a freezer-safe bag or storage container and is tightly sealed. You want to remove as much air as possible prior to freezing.
3. Make sure to label all of your freezer bags well. Always put the date you've prepared the bag on them so you know how long it's been in the freezer.
4. Use up your freezer meals within 2–3 months.
5. Consider portioning out your meals into single-serving sizes, or sizes large enough for your family.
6. Thaw them completely before cooking by placing them in the refrigerator for at least 24 hours. When reheating, you'll need the internal temperature to be 165°F.

Choosing a Slow Cooker

Not all slow cookers are created equal . . . or work equally well for everyone!

Those of us who use slow cookers frequently know we have our own preferences when it comes to which slow cooker we choose to use. For instance, I love my programmable slow cooker, but there are many programmable slow cookers I've tried that I've strongly disliked. Why? Because some go by increments of 15 or 30 minutes and some go by 4, 6, 8, or 10 hours. I dislike those restrictions, but I have family and friends who don't mind them at all! I am also pretty brand-loyal when it comes to my manual slow cookers because I've had great success with those and have had unsuccessful moments with slow cookers of other brands. So, which slow cooker(s) is/are best for your household?

It really depends on how many people you're feeding and if you're gone for long periods of time. Here are my recommendations:

For 2–3 person household	3–5 quart slow cooker
For 4–5 person household	5–6 quart slow cooker
For a 6+ person household	6½–7 quart slow cooker

Large slow cooker advantages/disadvantages:

Advantages:
- You can fit a loaf pan or a baking dish into a 6- or 7-quart, depending on the shape of your cooker. That allows you to make bread or cakes, or even smaller quantities of main dishes. (Take your favorite baking dish and loaf pan along when you shop for a cooker to make sure they'll fit inside.)
- You can feed large groups of people, or make larger quantities of food, allowing for leftovers, or meals, to freeze.

Disadvantages:
- They take up more storage room.
- They don't fit as neatly into a dishwasher.
- If your crock isn't ⅔–¾ full, you may burn your food.

Small slow cooker advantages/disadvantages:

Advantages:
- They're great for lots of appetizers, for serving hot drinks, for baking cakes straight in the crock, and for dorm rooms or apartments.
- Great option for making recipes of smaller quantities.

Disadvantages:
- Food in smaller quantities tends to cook more quickly than larger amounts. So keep an eye on it.
- Chances are, you won't have many leftovers. So, if you like to have leftovers, a smaller slow cooker may not be a good option for you.

My Recommendation:

Have at least two slow cookers; one around 3 to 4 quarts and one 6 quarts or larger. A third would be a huge bonus (and a great advantage to your cooking repertoire!). The advantage of having at least a couple is you can make a larger variety of recipes. Also, you can make at least two or three dishes at once for a whole meal.

Manual vs. Programmable

If you are gone for only six to eight hours a day, a manual slow cooker might be just fine for you. If you are gone for more than eight hours during the day, I would highly recommend purchasing a programmable slow cooker that will switch to Warm when the cook time you set is up. It will allow you to cook a wider variety of recipes.

The two I use most frequently are my 4-quart manual slow cooker and my 6½-quart programmable slow cooker. I like that I can make smaller portions in my 4-quart slow cooker on days I don't need or want leftovers, but I also love how my 6½-quart slow cooker can accommodate whole chickens, turkey breasts, hams, or big batches of soups. I use them both often.

Get to know your slow cooker . . .

Plan a little time to get acquainted with your slow cooker. Each slow cooker has its own personality—just like your oven (and your car). Plus, many new slow cookers cook hotter and faster than earlier models. I think that with all of the concern for food safety, the slow cooker manufacturers have amped up their settings so that "High," "Low," and "Warm" are all higher temperatures than in the older models. That means they cook hotter—and therefore, faster— than the first slow cookers. The beauty of these little machines is that they're supposed to cook low and slow. We count on that when we flip the switch in the morning before we leave the house for ten hours or so. So, because none of us knows what kind of temperament our slow cooker has until we try it out, nor how hot it cooks—don't assume anything. Save yourself a disappointment and make the first recipe in your new slow cooker on a day when you're at home. Cook it for the shortest amount of time the recipe calls for. Then, check the food to see if it's done. Or if you start smelling food that seems to be finished, turn off the cooker and rescue your food.

Also, all slow cookers seem to have a "hot spot," which is of great importance to know, especially when baking with your slow cooker. This spot may tend to burn food in that area if you're not careful. If you're baking directly in your slow cooker, I recommend covering the "hot spot" with some foil.

Take notes . . .

Don't be afraid to make notes in your cookbook. It's yours! Chances are, it will eventually get passed down to someone in your family and they will love and appreciate all of your musings. Take note of which slow cooker you used and exactly how long it took to cook the recipe. The next time you make it, you won't need to try to remember. Apply what you learned to the next recipes you make in your cooker. If another recipe says it needs to cook 7–9 hours, and you've discovered your slow cooker cooks on the faster side, cook that recipe for 6–6½ hours and then check it. You can always cook a recipe longer—but you can't reverse things if it's overdone.

Get creative . . .

If you know your morning is going to be hectic, prepare everything the night before, take it out so the crock warms up to room temperature when you first get up in the morning, then plug it in and turn it on as you're leaving the house.

If you want to make something that has a short cook time and you're going to be gone longer than that, cook it the night before and refrigerate it for the next day. Warm it up when you get home. Or, cook those recipes on the weekend when you know you'll be home and eat them later in the week.

Slow Cooking Tips and Tricks and Other Things You May Not Know

- Slow cookers tend to work best when they're ⅔ to ¾ of the way full. You may need to increase the cooking time if you've exceeded that amount, or reduce it if you've put in less than that. If you're going to exceed that limit, it would be best to reduce the recipe, or split it between two slow cookers. (Remember how I suggested owning at least two or three slow cookers?)
- Keep your veggies on the bottom. That puts them in more direct contact with the heat. The fuller your slow cooker, the longer it will take its contents to cook. Also, the more densely packed the cooker's contents are, the longer they will take to cook. And finally, the larger the chunks of meat or vegetables, the more time they will need to cook.
- Keep the lid on! Every time you take a peek, you lose 20 minutes of cooking time. Please take this into consideration each time you lift the lid! I know, some of you can't help yourself and are going to lift anyway. Just don't forget to tack on 20 minutes to your cook time for each time you peeked!
- Sometimes it's beneficial to remove the lid. If you'd like your dish to thicken a bit, take the lid off during the last half hour to hour of cooking time.
- If you have a big slow cooker (7- to 8-quart), you can cook a small batch in it by putting the recipe ingredients into an oven-safe baking dish or baking pan and then placing that into the cooker's crock. First, put a trivet or some metal jar rings on the bottom of the crock, and then set your dish or pan on top of them. Or a loaf pan may "hook onto" the top ridges of the crock belonging to a large oval cooker and hang there straight and securely, "baking" a cake or quick bread. Cover the cooker and flip it on.

- The outside of your slow cooker will be hot! Please remember to keep it out of reach of children and keep that in mind for yourself as well!
- Get yourself a quick-read meat thermometer and use it! This helps remove the question of whether or not your meat is fully cooked, and helps prevent you from overcooking your meat as well. Internal Cooking Temperatures:
  - Beef—125–130°F (rare); 140–145°F (medium); 160°F (well-done)
  - Pork—140–145°F (rare); 145–150°F (medium); 160°F (well-done)
  - Turkey and Chicken—165°F
  - Frozen meat: The basic rule of thumb is, don't put frozen meat into the slow cooker. The meat does not reach the proper internal temperature in time. This especially applies to thick cuts of meat! Proceed with caution!
- Add fresh herbs 10 minutes before the end of the cooking time to maximize their flavor.
- If your recipe calls for cooked pasta, add it 10 minutes before the end of the cooking time if the cooker is on High; 30 minutes before the end of the cooking time if it's on Low. Then the pasta won't get mushy.
- If your recipe calls for sour cream or cream, stir it in 5 minutes before the end of the cooking time. You want it to heat but not boil or simmer.
- Approximate Slow Cooker Temperatures (Remember, each slow cooker is different):
  - High—212–300°F
  - Low—170–200°F
  - Simmer—185°F
  - Warm—165°F
- Cooked and dried bean measurements:
  - 16-oz. can, drained = about 1¾ cups beans
  - 19-oz. can, drained = about 2 cups beans
  - 1 lb. dried beans (about 2½ cups) = 5 cups cooked beans

Breakfast

Ham Omelet

*10 Ing. or Fewer *Gluten-Free*

Kelly Bailey, Dillsburg, PA

Makes 12 servings

Prep. Time: 15 minutes ❦ Cooking Time: 7–9 hours ❦ Ideal slow-cooker size: 6-qt.

Needed at Time of Preparation:

1 lb. ham, chopped

1 onion, chopped

1 green bell pepper, chopped

1 cup sliced fresh mushrooms

12 eggs, beaten

1 Tbsp. thyme, basil, rosemary, or tarragon, depending on what you like

½ tsp. cayenne pepper

Preparation instructions:

1. Place all ingredients in a gallon-sized freezer bag.

2. Smoosh the ingredients in the bag until they're well blended.

3. Remove as much air as possible and seal bag.

4. Label the bag with the information below, then freeze.

Information for Freezer Bag:

HAM OMELET

Makes 12 servings

Cooking Time: 7–9 hours ❦ Ideal slow-cooker size: 6-qt.

Needed at Time of Cooking:

32-oz. bag frozen hash brown potatoes, or 5 cups cooked, shredded potatoes *choose the cooked, shredded potatoes to keep this recipe gluten-free

1 cup whole milk

2 cups shredded cheddar cheese

Instructions:

1. Thaw bag completely for 24–48 hours or more.

2. Spray crock with nonstick spray.

3. Place shredded potatoes in the bottom of the crock.

4. Pour contents of the freezer bag, milk, and shredded cheddar over the top of hash browns. Stir to combine well.

5. Cover and cook on Low 7–9 hours, until omelet is set in the middle and lightly browned at edges.

Fresh Veggie and Herb Omelet

*Gluten-Free *Vegetarian

Hope Comerford, Clinton Township, MI

Makes 8 servings

Prep. Time: 20 minutes ❧ Cooking Time: 4–6 hours ❧ Ideal slow-cooker size: 6-qt.

Needed at Time of Preparation:

12 eggs, beaten

½ tsp. kosher salt

¼ tsp. pepper

3 cloves garlic, minced

1 tsp. fresh chopped basil

6 dashes hot sauce

2 cups broccoli florets

1 yellow bell pepper, diced

1 red bell pepper, diced

1 onion, diced

Preparation Instructions:

1. In a gallon-sized freezer bag, place the eggs, salt, pepper, garlic, basil, and hot sauce. Smoosh until all the ingredients are well-mixed.

2. Place broccoli, yellow pepper, red pepper, and onion in the bag.

3. Remove as much air as possible and seal the bag.

4. Label the bag with the information below, then freeze.

Information for Freezer Bag:

FRESH VEGGIE AND HERB OMELET

Makes 8 servings

Cooking Time: 4–6 hours ❧ Ideal slow-cooker size: 6-qt.

Needed at Time of Cooking/Serving:

1 cup unsweetened almond milk or milk

1 cup crumbled feta cheese

1 cup diced cherry tomatoes

½ cup fresh chopped parsley

Instructions:

1. Thaw bag completely for 24–48 hours or more.

2. Spray crock with nonstick spray.

3. Pour milk into bag and smoosh until mixed well. Pour the contents into the crock.

4. Cover and cook on Low for 4–6 hours, or until center is set.

5. Sprinkle feta over the top, then cook an additional 30 minutes.

6. To serve, sprinkle the omelet with the chopped tomatoes and fresh parsley.

Italian Frittata

*10 Ing. or Fewer *Gluten-Free *Vegetarian–Optional

Hope Comerford, Clinton Township, MI

Makes 6 servings

Prep. Time: 10 minutes 🌿 Cooking Time: 3–4 hours 🌿 Ideal slow-cooker size: 5- or 6-qt.

Needed at Time of Preparation:

10 eggs, beaten

1 Tbsp. chopped fresh basil

1 Tbsp. chopped fresh mint

1 Tbsp. chopped fresh sage

1 Tbsp. chopped fresh oregano

½ tsp. sea salt

⅓ tsp. pepper

1 Tbsp. grated Parmesan cheese

¼ cup diced prosciutto (leave out to keep this recipe vegetarian)

½ cup chopped onion

Preparation instructions:

1. In a gallon-sized freezer bag, add all of the ingredients.

2. Smoosh the bag until the contents are well-mixed.

3. Remove as much air as possible and seal bag.

4. Label the bag with the information below, then freeze.

Information for Freezer Bag:

ITALIAN FRITTATA

Makes 6 servings

Cooking Time: 3–4 hours 🌿 Ideal slow-cooker size: 5- or 6-qt.

Instructions:

1. Thaw bag completely for 24–48 hours or more.
2. Spray your crock with nonstick spray.
3. Pour the contents of the bag into the crock.
4. Cover and cook on Low for 3–4 hours.

Breakfast Casserole

*5 Ing. or Fewer *Quick to Prep

Shirley Hinh, Wayland, IA

Makes 8–10 servings

Prep. Time: 15 minutes ❧ Cooking Time: 3 hours ❧ Ideal slow-cooker size: 4-qt.

Needed at Time of Preparation:

6 eggs, beaten

1 lb. miniature smoked sausage links, or
1½ lbs. bulk sausage,
browned and drained

1 tsp. salt

½ tsp. dry mustard

Preparation instructions:

1. In a gallon-sized freezer bag, add all of the ingredients.

2. Smoosh the contents of the bag until the ingredients are well-mixed.

3. Remove as much air as possible and seal bag.

4. Label the bag with the information below, then freeze.

Information for Freezer Bag:

BREAKFAST CASSEROLE

Makes 8–10 servings

Cooking Time: 3 hours ❧ Ideal slow-cooker size: 4-qt.

Needed at Time of Cooking:

1½ cups milk

1 cup shredded cheddar cheese

8 slices bread, torn into pieces

1 cup shredded mozzarella cheese

Instructions:

1. Thaw bag completely for 24–48 hours or more.

2. Pour the milk and shredded cheddar into the freezer bag and smoosh until well-combined.

3. Add the bread pieces to the bag, seal, and shake around until it's well coated.

4. Grease the crock with nonstick spray.

5. Pour the contents of the bag into the crock.

6. Sprinkle mozzarella cheese over top.

7. Cover and cook 2 hours on High, and then 1 hour on Low.

Breakfast Bake

*5 Ing. or Fewer *Quick to Prep *Gluten-Free*

Kristi See, Weskan, KS

Makes 10 servings

Prep. Time: 15 minutes ❦ Cooking Time: 3–4 hours ❦ Ideal slow-cooker size: 4- to 5-qt.

Needed at Time of Preparation:

12 eggs, beaten

1 cup diced cooked ham

1 tsp. salt

½ tsp. pepper

Preparation instructions:

1. In a gallon-sized freezer bag, add all ingredients.

2. Smoosh the bag until everything is well-blended.

3. Remove as much air as possible and seal the bag.

4. Label the bag with the information below, then freeze.

Information for Freezer Bag:

BREAKFAST BAKE

Makes 10 servings

Cooking Time: 3–4 hours ❦ Ideal slow-cooker size: 4- to 5-qt.

Needed at Time of Cooking:

1 cup milk

1½–2 cups grated cheese, your choice

Instructions:

1. Thaw bag completely for 24–48 hours or more.

2. Spray crock with nonstick spray.

3. Open bag and pour in milk and grated cheese. Smoosh until everything is well-combined.

4. Pour contents of the bag into the crock.

5. Cover and cook on Low 3–4 hours.

Fruity Oatmeal

*10 Ing. or Fewer *Gluten-Free–Optional *Vegetarian

Mary Stoltzfus, Manheim, PA

Makes 6–8 servings

Prep. Time: 10 minutes ❧ Cooking Time: 4–6 hours ❧ Ideal slow-cooker size: 4- to 5-qt.

Needed at Time of Preparation:

⅔ cup oil

1 cup sugar

2 eggs, lightly beaten

1½ cups milk

1 tsp. vanilla extract

4 cups quick oats *use gluten-free oats to keep this gluten-free

1 Tbsp. baking powder

1 tsp. salt

1 tsp. cinnamon

1–2 cups fresh or frozen fruit (blueberries, raspberries, peaches)

Preparation Instructions:

1. Combine oil, sugar, and eggs in a bowl. Mix in remaining ingredients, except fruit.

2. Gently stir in fruit.

3. Transfer batter to a gallon freezer bag.

4. Remove air, flatten bag, and seal.

5. Label the bag with the information below, then freeze.

Information for Freezer Bag:

FRUITY OATMEAL

Makes 6–8 servings

Cooking Time: 4–6 hours ❧ Ideal slow-cooker size: 4- to 5-qt.

Serving Suggestion: Goes well with fresh fruit and yogurt on top.

Instructions:

1. Thaw bag completely for 24–48 hours or more.

2. Spray crock with nonstick spray.

3. Empty contents of bag into crock, then cover and cook on Low for 4–6 hours.

4. Serve with optional fresh fruit and yogurt.

Apple Breakfast Risotto

*10 Ing. or Fewer *Gluten-Free *Vegetarian *Vegan–Optional

Hope Comerford, Clinton Township, MI

Makes 4 servings

Prep. Time: 10 minutes 🌿 Cooking Time: 8 hours 🌿 Ideal slow-cooker size: 3-qt.

Needed at Time of Preparation:

4 Granny Smith apples, peeled and sliced

2 cups apple juice

2 cups water

¼ cup brown sugar

1½ tsp. cinnamon

¼ tsp. salt

1 tsp. vanilla extract

⅛ tsp. cloves

⅛ tsp. nutmeg

4 Tbsp. butter, sliced (to keep vegan, replace with oil)

Preparation Instructions:

1. Place all ingredients into a gallon-sized freezer bag. Smoosh it all around to combine everything well.

2. Remove as much air as possible and seal bag.

3. Label the bag with the information below, then freeze.

Information for Freezer Bag:

APPLE BREAKFAST RISOTTO

Makes 4 servings 🌿 Cooking Time: 8 hours
Ideal slow-cooker size: 3-qt.

Needed at Time of Cooking:

2½ cups Arborio rice

Instructions:

1. Thaw bag completely for 24–48 hours or more.

2. Spray crock with nonstick spray.

3. Add the Arborio rice into the bag and smoosh until everything is combined well. Pour the contents of the bag into the crock.

4. Cover and cook on Low for 8 hours.

Breakfast Apple Cobbler

*5 Ing. or Fewer *Gluten-Free *Vegetarian *Vegan

Virginia Graybill, Hershey, PA

Makes 8–10 servings

Prep. Time: 20–25 minutes ⚘ *Cooking Time: 2–6 hours* ⚘ *Ideal slow-cooker size: 5- or 6-qt.*

Needed at Time of Preparation:

8 medium-sized tart apples, cored, peeled and sliced

½ cup sugar

2 Tbsp. fresh lemon juice

1–2 tsp. grated lemon rind

dash ground cinnamon

Preparation instructions:

1. Place all ingredients into a gallon-sized freezer bag, then smoosh around to coat everything evenly.

2. Remove as much air as possible and seal the bag.

3. Label the bag with the information below, then freeze.

Information for Freezer Bag:

BREAKFAST APPLE COBBLER

Makes 8–10 servings

Cooking Time: 2–6 hours ⚘ *Ideal slow-cooker size: 5- or 6-qt.*

Needed at Time of Cooking:

1½ cups natural fat-free cereal mixed with fruit and nuts (replace with a gluten-free substitute to keep this recipe gluten-free)

4 Tbsp. (½ stick) butter, melted

Instructions:

1. Thaw contents of bag completely for 24–48 hours or more.

2. Spray crock with nonstick spray.

3. Mix cereal and melted butter together.

4. Add contents of the bag into the slow cooker and spread out evenly. Spread the cereal/butter mixture over the top.

5. Cover. Cook on Low 6 hours, or on High 2–3 hours.

Chicken & Turkey Main Dishes

Honey Garlic Chicken

*5 Ing. or Fewer *Quick to Prep *Gluten-Free–Optional

Donna Treloar, Muncie, IN

Makes 4 servings

Prep. Time: 10 minutes ❧ *Cooking Time: 4 hours* ❧ *Ideal slow-cooker size: 5-qt.*

Needed at Time of Preparation:

4 boneless, skinless chicken thighs

⅓ cup honey

1 cup ketchup

2 Tbsp. soy sauce (replace with tamari or liquid aminos to keep this recipe gluten-free)

4 cloves garlic, minced

Preparation Instructions:

1. Place all ingredients into a gallon-sized freezer bag. Smoosh everything around to coat the chicken well.

2. Remove as much air as possible and seal the bag.

3. Label the bag with the information below, then freeze.

Information for Freezer Bag:

HONEY GARLIC CHICKEN

Makes 4 servings

Cooking Time: 4 hours ❧ *Ideal slow-cooker size: 5-qt.*

Serving Suggestion: Serve over cooked rice.

Instructions:

1. Thaw contents of bag completely for 24–48 hours or more.

2. Grease interior of slow-cooker crock.

3. Dump contents of the freezer bag into the crock.

4. Cover. Cook on Low 4 hours or until instant-read meat thermometer registers 160–165°F when inserted into center of thighs.

5. Serve chicken and sauce together over optional rice.

Soy Honey Chicken

*5 Ing. or Fewer *Quick to Prep *Gluten-Free–Optional*

Colleen Heatwole, Burton, MI

Makes 4 servings

Prep. Time: 10 minutes ❧ Cooking Time: 5 hours ❧ Ideal slow-cooker size: 3- to 5-quart

Needed at Time of Preparation:

½ cup soy sauce *replace with tamari or liquid aminos to keep this recipe gluten-free

¼ cup honey

2 Tbsp. crushed garlic

1 tsp. ground ginger

2½ pounds boneless, skinless chicken pieces

Preparation Instructions:

1. Warm soy sauce, honey, crushed garlic, and ground ginger together in microwave until honey is melted, about 1½ minutes.

2. In a gallon-sized freezer bag place the chicken pieces, pour the marinade over the top, and make sure chicken is evenly coated.

3. Remove as much air as possible and seal bag.

4. Label the bag with the information below, then freeze.

Information for Freezer Bag:

SOY HONEY CHICKEN

Makes 4 servings

Cooking Time: 5 hours ❧ Ideal slow-cooker size: 3- to 5-quart

Serving Suggestion: Serve with rice and a vegetable such as edamame.

Instructions:

1. Thaw bag completely for 24–48 hours or more.

2. Place contents of the freezer bag in a 3- to 5-quart slow cooker.

3. Cover and cook on Low 5 hours.

4. Serve with rice and edamame, if desired, or other vegetable.

Slow-Cooker Honey Mustard Chicken

Barbara Stutzman, Crossville, TN

Gluten-Free–Optional

Makes 6–8 servings

Prep. Time: 30 minutes ❧ Cooking Time: 4–5 hours ❧ Ideal slow-cooker size: 6-qt.

Needed at Time of Preparation:

2–3 lbs. boneless, skinless chicken thighs
1 large onion, sliced, about ½ cup
3 cloves garlic, sliced
2 Tbsp. honey
¼ cup Dijon mustard *check to make sure yours is gluten-free
1 Tbsp. coarse-grain mustard *check to make sure yours is gluten-free
2 Tbsp. red wine vinegar
2 tsp. olive oil
1 tsp. coarsely ground black pepper
pinch cayenne pepper
½ cup water

Preparation Instructions:

1. Place all ingredients into a gallon-sized freezer bag.
2. Smoosh bag around to coat chicken thighs evenly.
3. Remove as much air as possible and seal the bag.
4. Label the bag with the information below, then freeze.

TIP: If 6–8 servings is just too much for you, either split the recipe between 2 freezer bags or make it all and freeze the leftovers.

Information for Freezer Bag:

SLOW-COOKER HONEY MUSTARD CHICKEN

Makes 6–8 servings

Cooking Time: 4–5 hours ❧ Ideal slow-cooker size: 6-qt.

Needed at Time of Serving:

2 green onions, sliced on an angle, for garnish, *optional*

Instructions:

1. Thaw bag completely for 24–48 hours or more.
2. Grease crock.
3. Pour contents of bag in crock. If you need to add a second layer, stagger the pieces so they don't directly overlap each other.
4. Cover. Cook on Low 4–5 hours, or until instant-read meat thermometer registers 165°F when stuck into center of thighs.
5. Serve chicken topped with sauce, and garnish with green onions if you wish.

Chicken Dijon Dinner

*10 Ing. or Fewer *Gluten-Free–Optional

Barbara Stutzman, Crossville, TN

Makes 4–6 servings

Prep. Time: 20 minutes ❧ Cooking Time: 4 hours ❧ Ideal slow-cooker size: 6-qt.

Needed at Time of Preparation:

2 lbs. boneless, skinless chicken thighs

2 cloves garlic, minced

1 Tbsp. olive oil

6 Tbsp. white wine vinegar

4 Tbsp. soy sauce *replace with tamari or liquid aminos to make this recipe gluten-free

4 Tbsp. Dijon mustard *check to make sure yours is gluten-free to make this recipe gluten-free

1 lb. sliced mushrooms

Preparation Instructions:

1. Place all ingredients in a gallon-sized freezer bag.

2. Smoosh bag around to coat everything evenly.

3. Remove as much air as possible and seal bag.

4. Label the bag with the information below, then freeze.

Information for Freezer Bag:

CHICKEN DIJON DINNER

Makes 4–6 servings

Cooking Time: 4 hours ❧ Ideal slow-cooker size: 6-qt.

Instructions:

1. Thaw bag completely for 24–48 hours or more.

2. Grease interior of crock.

3. Cover. Cook on Low for 4 hours, or until instant-read meat thermometer registers 160°F when stuck in center of chicken.

4. Serve chicken topped with sauce.

Simple Savory Chicken

*10 Ing. or Fewer *Gluten-Free

Hope Comerford, Clinton Township, MI

Makes 4–6 servings

Prep. Time: 5–8 minutes ❦ Cooking Time: 7–8 hours ❦ Ideal slow-cooker size: 3-qt.

Needed at Time of Preparation:

2 lbs. skinless chicken leg quarters

¼ cup chopped onion

2 cloves garlic, minced

1 tsp. basil

1 tsp. dill

½ tsp. salt

¼ tsp. black pepper

1 cup water

2 Tbsp. apple cider vinegar

Preparation Instructions:

1. Place all ingredients in a gallon-sized freezer bag.

2. Smoosh things around so everything is evenly coated in the bag.

3. Remove as much air as possible and seal bag.

4. Label the bag with the information below, then freeze.

Information for Freezer Bag:

SIMPLE SAVORY CHICKEN

Makes 4–6 servings

Cooking Time: 7–8 hours ❦ Ideal slow-cooker size: 3-qt.

Instructions:

1. Thaw bag completely for 24–48 hours or more.

2. Place all contents of the freezer bag into the crock.

3. Cover and cook on Low for 7–8 hours.

Garlic Mushroom Thighs

*10 Ing. or Fewer *Gluten-Free

Elaine Vigoda, Rochester, NY

Makes 6 servings

Prep. Time: 15 minutes   ❧   Cooking Time: 4 hours   ❧   Ideal slow-cooker size: 5-qt.

Needed at Time of Preparation:

6 boneless, skinless chicken thighs

8–10 cloves garlic, peeled and very lightly crushed

1 Tbsp. olive oil

¾ lb. fresh mushrooms, any combination of varieties, cut into bite-sized pieces

⅓ cup balsamic vinegar

1¼ cups gluten-free chicken broth or stock

1–2 bay leaves

½ tsp. dried thyme or 4 sprigs fresh thyme

2 tsp. apricot preserves (low-sugar or no-sugar-added preferred)

Preparation Instructions:

1. Add all ingredients to a gallon-sized freezer bag.

2. Remove as much air as possible and seal bag.

3. Label the bag with the information below, then freeze.

Information for Freezer Bag:

GARLIC MUSHROOM THIGHS

Makes 6 servings

Cooking Time: 4 hours   ❧   Ideal slow-cooker size: 5-qt.

Serving Suggestion: Serve over cooked spaghetti squash.

Instructions:

1. Thaw bag completely for 24–48 hours or more.

2. Grease interior of slow cooker.

3. Cover and cook on Low for 4 hours, or until an instant-read thermometer registers 160–165°F when stuck into the thighs.

4. Serve meat topped with vegetables with sauce spooned over.

5. Serve over cooked spaghetti squash, if desired.

Marinated Chicken Bites

*10 Ing. or Fewer *Gluten-Free

June Hackenberger, Thompsontown, PA

Makes 6–8 servings

Prep. Time: 5-10 minutes ❧ *Cooking Time: 3½–4 hours* ❧ *Ideal slow-cooker size: 4-qt.*

Needed at Time of Preparation:

½ cup soy sauce

¼ cup oil

¼ cup apple cider vinegar

1 tsp. oregano

½ tsp. basil

¼ tsp. garlic powder

¼ tsp. parsley

¼ tsp. black pepper

2 lbs. boneless, skinless chicken breast

Preparation Instructions:

1. Combine all ingredients except chicken in freezer bag. Seal and shake to combine.

2. Add chicken to bag.

3. Remove as much air as possible and seal bag.

4. Label with the information below, then freeze.

TIP: If 6–8 servings is just too much for you, either split the recipe between 2 freezer bags or make it all and freeze the leftovers.

Information for Freezer Bag:

MARINATED CHICKEN BITES

Makes 6–8 servings

Cooking Time: 3½–4 hours ❧ *Ideal slow-cooker size: 4-qt.*

Serving Suggestion: Serve with garlic bread and salad. *omit garlic bread to keep this recipe gluten-free

Instructions:

1. Thaw bag completely for 24–48 hours or more.

2. Place contents of bag in slow cooker and cook for 3½–4 hours on Low.

3. Cut chicken into serving-sized pieces and serve with salad and garlic bread, if desired.

Cranberry Chili Chicken

*5 Ing. or Fewer *Quick to Prep

Kelly Bailey, Mechanicsburg, PA

Makes 6 servings

Prep. Time: 10 minutes ❦ Cooking Time: 4 hours ❦ Ideal slow-cooker size: 5-qt.

Needed at Time of Preparation:

6 boneless, skinless chicken thighs

½ cup chili sauce

2 Tbsp. orange marmalade

½ cup whole-berry cranberry sauce

¼ tsp. ground allspice

Preparation Instructions:

1. Place all ingredients into a gallon-sized freezer bag.

2. Smoosh everything around to coat chicken completely.

3. Remove as much air as possible and seal bag.

4. Label the bag with the information below, then freeze.

Information for Freezer Bag:

CRANBERRY CHILI CHICKEN

Makes 6 servings

Cooking Time: 4 hours ❦ Ideal slow-cooker size: 5-qt.

Instructions:

1. Thaw bag completely for 24–48 hours or more.

2. Grease interior of slow-cooker crock.

3. Empty entire contents of bag into crock.

4. Cover. Cook on Low 4 hours, or until instant-read meat thermometer registers 160–165°F when stuck into thighs.

5. Serve thighs topped with the sauce.

Pineapple Chicken

*10 Ing. or Fewer *Quick to Prep *Gluten-Free–Optional

Amanda Gross, Souderton, PA

Makes 3–4 servings

Prep. Time: 5 minutes ❦ Cooking Time: 4–8 hours ❦ Ideal slow-cooker size: 7-qt.

Needed at Time of Preparation:

3–4 boneless, skinless chicken breast

¼ cup soy sauce *replace with tamari or liquid aminos to keep this recipe gluten-free

½ cup pineapple juice

½ cup ketchup

2 Tbsp. white vinegar

16 oz. crushed pineapple

Preparation Instructions:

1. Place all ingredients into a gallon-sized freezer bag.

2. Remove as much air as possible and seal bag.

3. Label the bag with the information below, then freeze.

TIP: This recipe is so easy to assemble, it may be worth doubling all ingredients now and making 2 freezer-bag meals for yourself instead of just 1.

Information for Freezer Bag:

PINEAPPLE CHICKEN

Makes 3–4 servings

Cooking Time: 4–8 hours ❦ Ideal slow-cooker size: 7-qt.

Serving Suggestion: Serve with rice.

Instructions:

1. Thaw bag completely for 24–48 hours or more.

2. Place all ingredients from freezer bag into slow cooker.

3. Cover and cook on High 4 hours or on Low 6–8 hours.

4. Serve over rice if you choose.

Orange Garlic Chicken

*5 Ing. or Fewer *Quick to Prep *Gluten-Free

Susan Kasting, Jenks, OK

Makes 6 servings

Prep. Time: 15 minutes ❦ Cooking Time: 2½–6 hours ❦ Ideal slow-cooker size: 4-qt.

Needed at Time of Preparation:

1½ tsp. dried thyme

6 cloves garlic, minced

6 skinless bone-in chicken breast halves

1 cup orange juice concentrate

2 Tbsp. balsamic vinegar

Preparation Instructions:

1. Place all ingredients into a gallon-sized freezer bag.

2. Remove as much air as possible and seal bag.

3. Label the bag with the information below, then freeze.

Information for Freezer Bag:

ORANGE GARLIC CHICKEN

Makes 6 servings

Cooking Time: 2½–6 hours ❦ Ideal slow-cooker size: 4-qt.

Instructions:

1. Thaw bag completely for 24–48 hours or more.

2. Empty contents of freezer bag into crock.

3. Cover and cook on Low 5–6 hours, or on High 2½–3 hours, or until chicken is tender but not dry.

Cranberry Chicken Barbecue

*10 Ing. or Fewer *Gluten-Free–Optional

Gladys M. High, Ephrata, PA

Makes 6–8 servings

Prep. Time: 10 minutes ❦ Cooking Time: 4–8 hours ❦ Ideal slow-cooker size: 4- to 5-qt.

Needed at Time of Preparation:

4 lbs. chicken pieces

½ tsp. salt

¼ tsp. pepper

16-oz. can whole-berry cranberry sauce *double-check to make sure yours is gluten-free to keep this recipe gluten-free

1 cup barbecue sauce *choose a gluten-free barbecue sauce to make this recipe gluten-free

½ cup diced celery, *optional*

½ cup diced onion, *optional*

Preparation Instructions:

1. Place all ingredients into a gallon-sized freezer bag.

2. Smoosh everything around to coat everything well.

3. Remove as much air as possible and seal bag.

4. Label the bag with the information below, then freeze.

TIP: If 6–8 servings is just too much for you, either split the recipe between 2 freezer bags or make it all and freeze the leftovers.

Information for Freezer Bag:

CRANBERRY CHICKEN BARBECUE

Makes 6–8 servings

Cooking Time: 4–8 hours ❦ Ideal slow-cooker size: 4- to 5-qt.

Instructions:

1. Thaw bag completely for 24–48 hours or more.

2. Empty contents of freezer bag into crock.

3. Cover and cook on High 4 hours, or on Low 6–8 hours, or until chicken is tender but not dry.

Zesty Barbecued Chicken

Carol Eberly, Harrisonburg, VA

*10 Ing. or Fewer *Gluten-Free–Optional

Makes 8–12 servings

Prep. Time: 10–15 minutes ❦ Cooking Time: 4–5 hours ❦ Ideal slow-cooker size: 6-qt.

Needed at Time of Preparation:

8–12 boneless, skinless chicken thighs

3 Tbsp. ketchup

2 Tbsp. Worcestershire sauce *make sure yours is gluten-free if you're making this recipe gluten-free

2 Tbsp. apple cider vinegar

2 Tbsp. soy sauce *replace with tamari or liquid aminos if you're making this recipe gluten-free

3 Tbsp. brown sugar

1 tsp. spicy brown mustard *make sure yours is gluten-free if you're making this recipe gluten-free

1 tsp. salt

1 tsp. black pepper

Preparation Instructions:

1. Place all ingredients into a gallon-sized freezer bag. Smoosh around to coat everything evenly.

2. Remove as much air as possible and seal bag.

3. Label the bag with the information below, then freeze.

TIP: If 8–12 servings is just too much for you, either split the recipe between 2–3 freezer bags or make it all and freeze the leftovers.

Information for Freezer Bag:

ZESTY BARBECUED CHICKEN

Makes 8–12 servings

Cooking Time: 4–5 hours ❦ Ideal slow-cooker size: 6-qt.

Instructions:

1. Thaw bag completely for 24–48 hours or more.

2. Grease interior of slow-cooker crock.

3. Empty contents of freezer bag into crock.

4. Cover. Cook on Low 4–5 hours, or until instant-read meat thermometer registers 160–165°F when stuck into thighs.

BBQ Chicken Sandwiches

*10 Ing. or Fewer *Gluten-Free–Optional*

Sarah Herr, Goshen, IN

Makes 8 servings

Prep. Time: 15 minutes ❦ Cooking Time: 4 hours ❦ Ideal slow-cooker size: 5-qt.

Needed at Time of Preparation:

3 lbs. boneless, skinless chicken thighs

1 onion, chopped

½ cup brown sugar

½ cup apple cider vinegar

½ cup ketchup

1 tsp. ground mustard *make sure yours is gluten-free if you're making this recipe gluten-free

1 tsp. cumin

1 Tbsp. chili powder

½ tsp. black pepper

Preparation Instructions:

1. Place all ingredients into a gallon-sized freezer bag. Smoosh around to coat everything evenly.

2. Remove as much air as possible and seal bag.

3. Label the bag with the information below, then freeze.

TIP: If 8 servings is just too much for you, either split the recipe between 2 freezer bags or make it all and freeze the leftovers.

Information for Freezer Bag:

BBQ CHICKEN SANDWICHES

Makes 8 servings

Cooking Time: 4 hours ❦ Ideal slow-cooker size: 5-qt.

Needed at Time of Serving:

8 hamburger buns *replace with gluten-free buns if making this recipe gluten-free

Instructions:

1. Thaw bag completely for 24–48 hours or more.

2. Grease interior of slow-cooker crock.

3. Empty contents of freezer bag into crock, spreading out evenly.

4. Cover. Cook on Low 4 hours, or until instant-read meat thermometer registers 160°F when stuck in center of thighs.

5. Lift cooked chicken out of crock and shred with 2 forks.

6. Stir shredded meat back into sauce in crock.

7. Serve on hamburger buns.

Barbecue Chicken for Sandwiches

*10 Ing. or Fewer *Quick to Prep *Gluten-Free–Optional*

Amanda Gross, Souderton, PA

Makes 4–6 sandwiches

Prep. Time: 5 minutes 🌱 Cooking Time: 4–6 hours 🌱 Ideal slow-cooker size: 7-qt.

Needed at Time of Preparation:

4 boneless, skinless chicken breast

18 oz. barbecue sauce of choice *make sure yours is gluten-free if you're making this recipe gluten-free

¼ cup white vinegar

¼ tsp. cayenne pepper

½ tsp. onion powder

¼ cup brown sugar

1 tsp. garlic powder

Preparation Instructions:

1. Combine all ingredients in a gallon-sized freezer bag.

2. Massage together everything in bag.

3. Remove as much air as possible and seal bag.

4. Label the bag with the information below, then freeze.

Information for Freezer Bag:

BARBECUE CHICKEN FOR SANDWICHES

Makes 4–6 sandwiches

Cooking Time: 4–6 hours 🌱 Ideal slow-cooker size: 7-qt.

Needed at Time of Serving:

4–6 sandwich rolls *replace with gluten-free sandwich rolls to keep this recipe gluten-free

Instructions:

1. Thaw bag completely for 24–48 hours or more.

2. Empty entire contents of bag into crock.

3. Cover and coook on Low 4–6 hours.

4. During the last 30 minutes, shred chicken with a fork, then continue cooking.

5. Serve in sandwich rolls.

Sweet-and-Sour Chicken

Gluten-Free–Optional Makes 6–8 servings

Janette Fox, Honey Brook, PA

Prep. Time: 15 minutes ❧ Cooking Time: 4 hours ❧ Ideal slow-cooker size: 5-qt.

Needed at Time of Preparation:

3 lbs. boneless, skinless chicken thighs

½ cup chopped onions

½ green pepper, chopped

15-oz. can pineapple chunks with juice

¾–1 cup reserved pineapple juice

¾ cup ketchup

¼ cup brown sugar, packed

2 Tbsp. apple cider vinegar

2 tsp. soy sauce *replace with tamari or liquid aminos to make this recipe gluten-free

½ tsp. garlic salt

½ tsp. salt

¼ tsp. black pepper

Preparation Instructions:

1. Place all ingredients into a gallon-sized freezer bag. Smoosh around to coat everything evenly.

2. Remove as much air as possible and seal bag.

3. Label the bag with the information below, then freeze.

TIP: If 6–8 servings is just too much for you, either split the recipe between 2 freezer bags or make it all and freeze the leftovers.

Information for Freezer Bag:

SWEET-AND-SOUR CHICKEN

Makes 6–8 servings

Cooking Time: 4 hours ❧ Ideal slow-cooker size: 5-qt.

Needed at Time of Serving:

cooked rice

Instructions:

1. Thaw bag completely for 24–48 hours or more.

2. Grease interior of slow-cooker crock.

3. Empty contents of freezer bag into crock, spreading everything out evenly.

4. Cover. Cook on Low 4 hours, or until instant-read meat thermometer registers 165°F when stuck into center of thighs.

5. Serve over cooked rice.

Asian-Style Chicken with Pineapple

*10 Ing. or Fewer *Gluten-Free*

Andrea Maher, Dunedin, FL

Makes 6 servings

Prep. Time: 10 minutes 🌿 Cooking Time: 3–8 hours 🌿 Ideal slow-cooker size: 5- or 6-qt.

Needed at Time of Preparation:

24 oz. boneless, skinless chicken breast, cut into bite size pieces

3 cups pineapple, cubed

¼ cup Bragg liquid aminos

1 Tbsp. brown sugar

½ cup chopped onion or 2 Tbsp. onion powder

1 cup low-sodium gluten-free chicken broth or stock

½ tsp. ground ginger

Preparation Instructions:

1. Place all ingredients into a gallon-sized freezer bag and smoosh around to coat everything evenly.

2. Remove as much air as possible and seal bag.

3. Label the bag with the information below, then freeze.

Information for Freezer Bag:

ASIAN-STYLE CHICKEN WITH PINEAPPLE

Makes 6 servings

Cooking Time: 3–8 hours 🌿 Ideal slow-cooker size: 5- or 6-qt.

Needed at Time of Cooking:

2 16-oz. bags frozen Szechuan mixed veggies or any mixed veggies

Instructions:

1. Thaw bag completely for 24–48 hours or more.

2. Dump the contents of the freezer bag into the crock and spread out evenly.

3. Cover and cook on High 3–4 hours or Low 6–8 hours. Add frozen veggies in the last 1–2 hours.

Memories of Tucson Chicken

Gluten-Free–Optional

Joanna Harrison, Lafayette, CO

Makes 6 servings

Prep. Time: 20 minutes ❧ Cooking Time: 4 hours ❧ Ideal slow-cooker size: 6-qt.

Needed at Time of Preparation:

1 medium onion, chopped coarsely

3 cloves garlic, minced

2–3 green chiles, chopped, or 4-oz. can chopped green chiles

1 cup chopped tomatoes

2 cups corn, fresh, frozen, or canned

2 tsp. dried oregano

1 tsp. ground cumin

1 tsp. dried basil

2 cups chicken broth *make sure yours is gluten-free if you're making this recipe gluten-free

6 boneless, skinless chicken thighs

Preparation Instructions:

1. Place all ingredients into a gallon-sized freezer bag.

2. Remove as much air as possible and seal bag.

3. Label the bag with the information below, then freeze.

Information for Freezer Bag:

MEMORIES OF TUCSON CHICKEN

Makes 6 servings

Cooking Time: 4 hours ❧ Ideal slow-cooker size: 6-qt.

Needed at Time of Cooking:

1 green bell pepper, chopped

1 or 2 zucchini, chopped

¼–½ cup cilantro leaves

Instructions:

1. Thaw bag completely for 24–48 hours or more.
2. Grease interior of slow-cooker crock.
3. Empty contents of freezer bag into crock and spread out evenly.
4. Cover. Cook on Low 3 hours.
5. Lift out thighs and keep covered on platter.
6. Stir in bell pepper and zucchini.
7. Return chicken to cooker, again pushing the pieces down into the liquid.
8. Cover and continue cooking 1 more hour on Low, or until an instant-read meat thermometer registers 160–165°F when stuck in the thighs.
9. Place the chicken on a platter. Spoon vegetables and broth over top. Scatter cilantro leaves over all and serve.

Chicken Cacciatore with Vegetables

*10 Ing. or Fewer *Gluten-Free

Marla Folkerts, Batavia, IL

Makes 4 servings

Prep. Time: 25 minutes ❧ *Cooking Time: 4 hours* ❧ *Ideal slow-cooker size: 5-qt.*

Needed at Time of Preparation:

2 lbs. boneless, skinless chicken thighs

28-oz. can diced tomatoes

½ red bell pepper and ½ green bell pepper, cut lengthwise

½ large onion, chopped

1 tsp. dried oregano

1 bay leaf

salt and pepper to taste

1-lb. bag baby carrots

Preparation Instructions:

1. Place all ingredients into a gallon-sized freezer bag and smoosh around so everything is evenly coated.

2. Remove as much air as possible and seal bag.

3. Label the bag with the information below, then freeze.

Information for Freezer Bag:

CHICKEN CACCIATORE WITH VEGETABLES

Makes 4 servings

Cooking Time: 4 hours ❧ *Ideal slow-cooker size: 5-qt.*

Needed at Time of Cooking:

3–4 large potatoes, chopped into chunks

Instructions:

1. Thaw bag completely for 24–48 hours or more.

2. Grease interior of slow-cooker crock.

3. Place potatoes and contents of freezer bag into crock. Stir.

4. Cover. Cook on Low for 4 hours, or until instant-read meat thermometer registers 160°F when stuck into center of meat, and veggies are as tender as you like them.

5. Remove bay leaf before serving.

Quick Italian Chicken Strips with Veggies

*5 Ing. or Fewer *Quick to Prep *Gluten-Free–Optional*

June Hackenberger, Thompsontown, PA

Makes 6 servings

Prep. Time: 10 minutes ❧ Cooking Time: 3½–4 hours ❧ Ideal slow-cooker size: 5- to 6-qt.

Needed at Time of Preparation:

1½ lbs. boneless, skinless chicken breast

2 lbs. frozen California blend vegetables

1 medium onion, chopped

3 cups Italian dressing *make sure yours is gluten-free if you're making this recipe gluten-free

Preparation Instructions:

1. Cut chicken breast in 1½-inch strips.

2. Place chicken, frozen vegetables, and onion into a gallon-sized freezer bag.

3. Pour dressing over top.

4. Remove as much air as possible and seal bag.

5. Label the bag with the information below, then freeze.

TIP: This recipe is so easy to assemble, you may consider doubling the ingredients and prepping 2 freezer-bag meals instead of just 1.

Information for Freezer Bag

QUICK ITALIAN CHICKEN STRIPS WITH VEGGIES

Makes 6 servings

Cooking Time: 3½–4 hours ❧ Ideal slow-cooker size: 5- to 6-qt.

Serving Suggestion: Serve with garlic bread. *omit if making this gluten-free

Instructions:

1. Thaw completely for 24–48 hours or more.

2. Place contents of bag into crock.

3. Cover and cook on Low for 3½–4 hours.

4. Serve with optional garlic bread.

Easy Slow-Cooker Italian Chicken

*5 Ing. or Fewer *Quick to Prep

Gwendolyn Muholland, Corryton, TN

Makes 4–6 servings

Prep. Time: 5–20 minutes ❦ Cooking Time: 4–8 hours ❦ Ideal slow-cooker size: 4-qt.

Needed at Time of Preparation:

2–3 boneless, skinless chicken breasts

23½-oz. jar Prego Traditional Italian sauce

14½-oz. jar Prego Homestyle Alfredo sauce

Preparation Instructions:

1. Place all ingredients into a gallon-sized freezer bag.

2. Remove as much air as possible and seal bag.

3. Label the bag with the information below, then freeze.

TIP: This recipe is so easy to assemble, you may consider doubling the ingredients now and prepping 2 freezer meals, instead of just 1.

Information for Freezer Bag:

EASY SLOW-COOKER ITALIAN CHICKEN

Makes 4–6 servings

Cooking Time: 4–8 hours ❦ Ideal slow-cooker size: 4-qt.

Needed at Time of Cooking/ Serving:

1 cup shredded mozzarella cheese

16-oz. box pasta, cooked according to instructions on box

Instructions:

1. Thaw bag completely for 24–48 hours or more.

2. Empty contents of the freezer bag into the crock. Top with the mozzarella cheese.

3. Cover and cook on Low for 6–8 hours or High for 4 hours.

4. When you're ready to eat, cook pasta according to the directions on the package.

5. Serve chicken on top of pasta with sauce.

Creamy Italian Chicken

*5 Ing. or Fewer *Quick to Prep

Amanda Gross, Souderton, PA

Makes 4 servings

Prep. Time: 5 minutes ❦ Cooking Time: 3–8 hours ❦ Ideal slow-cooker size: 7-qt.

Needed at Time of Preparation:

10¾-oz. can cream of chicken condensed soup

8 oz. cream cheese

1 oz. dry Italian dressing spices

2 lbs. boneless, skinless chicken breast

Preparation Instructions:

1. Place all ingredients in a gallon-sized freezer bag.

2. Remove as much air as possible and seal bag.

3. Label the bag with the information below, then freeze.

TIP: This recipe is so easy to assemble, you might consider doubling the ingredients and making 2 freezer meals while you're at it, instead of just 1.

Information for Freezer Bag:

CREAMY ITALIAN CHICKEN

Makes 4 servings

Cooking Time: 3–8 hours ❦ Ideal slow-cooker size: 7-qt.

Serving Suggestion: Great served with cooked noodles

Instructions:

1. Thaw completely for 24–48 hours or more.

2. Empty contents of freezer bag in crock and spread out evenly.

3. Cover and cook on High 3–4 hours or on Low 6–8 hours.

4. Serve over cooked noodles, if desired.

Italian Slow-Cooker Chicken

*10 Ing. or Fewer *Quick to Prep *Gluten-Free

Andrea Maher, Dunedin, FL

Makes 6 servings

Prep. Time: 5 minutes ❦ Cooking Time: 3–8 hours ❦ Ideal slow-cooker size: 6-qt.

Needed at Time of Preparation:

24 oz. boneless, skinless chicken breast, cut into small pieces

3 cups dried garbanzo beans

16-oz. bag frozen spinach

2 cups mushrooms, sliced

2 Tbsp. Mrs. Dash Italian Medley Seasoning Blend

1 cup low-sodium gluten-free chicken broth

Preparation Instructions:

1. Place all ingredients into a gallon-sized freezer bag.

2. Remove as much air as possible and seal bag.

3. Label the bag with the information below, then freeze.

TIP: This recipe is so easy to assemble, you may want to consider doubling the ingredients now and make 2 freezer-bag meals instead of just 1.

Information for Freezer Bag:

ITALIAN SLOW-COOKER CHICKEN

Makes 6 servings

Cooking Time: 3–8 hours ❦ Ideal slow-cooker size: 6-qt.

Instructions:

1. Thaw completely for 24–48 hours or more.

2. Empty contents of freezer bag into crock.

3. Cover and cook on Low for 6–8 hours or High for 3–4 hours.

Salsa Ranch Chicken with Black Beans

*10 Ing. or Fewer *Quick to Prep

Hope Comerford, Clinton Township, MI

Makes 8–10 servings

Prep. Time: 5 minutes   ❦   Cooking Time: 5–6 hours   ❦   Ideal slow-cooker size: 5-qt.

Need at Time of Preparation:

2–3 lbs. boneless, skinless chicken breasts

1¼-oz. pkg. taco seasoning

1-oz. pkg. dry ranch dressing mix

1 cup salsa

10¾-oz. can cream of chicken soup

15½-oz. can black beans, drained and rinsed

Preparation Instructions:

1. Place all ingredients into a gallon-sized freezer bag and smoosh around until everything is well coated.

2. Remove as much air as possible and seal bag.

3. Label the bag with the information below, then freeze.

TIP: If 8–10 servings is just too much for you, either split the recipe between 2 freezer bags or make it all and freeze the leftovers.

Information for Freezer Bag:

SALSA RANCH CHICKEN WITH BLACK BEANS

Makes 8–10 servings

Cooking Time: 5–6 hours   ❦   Ideal slow-cooker size: 5-qt.

Serving Suggestion: This is great in tacos, on nachos, on top of a salad, on top of rice, or just on its own!

Instructions:

1. Thaw bag completely for 24–48 hours or more.

2. Pour contents of freezer bag into crock and spread out evenly.

3. Cover and cook on Low for 5–6 hours.

4. Remove the chicken and shred it between two forks. Replace the chicken back in the crock and stir.

Southwestern Shredded Chicken

*10 Ing. or Fewer *Quick to Prep *Gluten-Free

Hope Comerford, Clinton Township, MI

Makes 4 servings

Prep. Time: 8–10 minutes ❧ Cooking Time: 5–6 hours ❧ Ideal slow-cooker size: 3-qt.

Needed at Time of Preparation:

1½ lbs. boneless, skinless chicken breast

1 Tbsp. chili powder

2 tsp. garlic powder

1 tsp. cumin

1 tsp. onion powder

½ tsp. kosher salt

¼ tsp. pepper

1 medium onion, chopped

14½-oz. can diced tomatoes

4-oz. can diced green chiles

Preparation Instructions:

1. Place all ingredients into a gallon-sized freezer bag and smoosh around until everything is mixed and coated.

2. Remove as much air as possible and seal bag.

3. Label the bag with the information below, then freeze.

Information for Freezer Bag:

SOUTHWESTERN SHREDDED CHICKEN

Makes 4 servings

Cooking Time: 5–6 hours ❧ Ideal slow-cooker size: 3-qt.

Needed at Time of Cooking:

½ cup nonfat Greek yogurt

optional toppings: lettuce, shredded cheese, Greek yogurt, and salsa

Serving Suggestions: Serve this over brown rice or quinoa topped with some shredded lettuce, shredded cheese, and fresh salsa.

Instructions:

1. Thaw bag completely for 24–48 hours or more.

2. Empty contents of freezer bag into crock and spread out.

3. Cover and cook on Low for 5–6 hours.

4. Turn your slow cooker to Warm. Remove the chicken and shred it between 2 forks.

5. Slowly whisk in the nonfat Greek yogurt with the juices in the crock. Replace the chicken in the crock and stir to mix in the juices.

Easy Enchilada Shredded Chicken

*10 Ing. or Fewer *Quick to Prep *Gluten-Free–Optional

Hope Comerford, Clinton Township, MI

Makes 10–14 servings

Prep. Time: 5 minutes 🍃 Cooking Time: 5–6 hours 🍃 Ideal slow-cooker size: 3- or 5-qt.

Needed at Time of Preparation:

5–6 lbs. boneless, skinless chicken breast

14½-oz. can petite diced tomatoes

1 medium onion, chopped

8 oz. red enchilada sauce *choose a gluten-free brand if you're making this recipe gluten-free

½ tsp. salt

½ tsp. chili powder

½ tsp. basil

½ tsp. garlic powder

¼ tsp. pepper

Preparation Instructions:

1. Place all ingredients in a gallon-sized freezer bag and smoosh around until everything is mixed and coated.

2. Remove as much air as possible and seal bag.

3. Label the bag with the information below, then freeze.

TIP: If 10–14 servings is just too much for you, either split the recipe between 2–4 freezer bags or make it all and freeze the leftovers into portions appropriate for your family.

Information for Freezer Bag:

EASY ENCHILADA SHREDDED CHICKEN

Makes 10–14 servings

Cooking Time: 5–6 hours 🍃 Ideal slow-cooker size: 3- or 5-qt.

Needed at Time of Serving:

A dollop of plain yogurt and a sprinkle of fresh cilantro, *optional*

Serving suggestion: Serve over salad, brown rice, quinoa, sweet potatoes, or nachos or in soft corn tortillas.

Instructions:

1. Thaw bag completely for 24–48 hours or more.

2. Empty contents of freezer bag into crock and spread out evenly.

3. Cover and cook on Low for 5–6 hours.

4. Remove chicken and shred it between two forks. Place the shredded chicken back in the crock and stir to mix in the juices.

5. Serve with the yogurt and cilantro, if desired, in one of the suggested ways.

Slow-Cooker Chicken Fajitas

*10 Ing. or Fewer *Gluten-Free–Optional

Lisa Clark, Chesterfield, MI

Makes 6–8 servings

Prep. Time: 20 minutes 🌿 Cooking Time: 3–8 hours 🌿 Ideal slow-cooker size: 3-qt.

Needed at Time of Preparation:

2 lbs. boneless, skinless chicken breasts

2 peppers, sliced (red, green, or yellow)

1 large onion, sliced

1 envelope taco seasoning
*choose a gluten-free brand to
keep this recipe gluten-free

10-oz. can Ro*Tel or plain diced
tomatoes

juice of 1 lime

Preparation Instructions:

1. Place all ingredients into a gallon-sized freezer bag and smoosh around to coat everything and mix.

2. Remove as much air as possible and seal bag.

3. Label the bag with the information below, then freeze.

TIP: If 6–8 servings is just too much for you, either split the recipe between 2 freezer bags or make it all and freeze the leftovers.

Information for Freezer Bag:

SLOW-COOKER CHICKEN FAJITAS

Makes 6–8 servings

Cooking Time: 3–8 hours 🌿 Ideal slow-cooker size: 3-qt.

Serving Suggestion: This pairs well with white rice, Spanish rice, or refried beans.

Instructions:

1. Thaw bag completely for 24–48 hours or more.

2. Empty contents of freezer bag into crock.

3. Cover and cook on Low 7–8 hours or High 3–4 hours.

4. If you prefer, you can shred chicken before serving or serve sliced.

Taco Chicken Bowls

*Quick to Prep *Gluten-Free–Optional*

Kayla Snyder, Saegertown, PA

Makes 8 servings

Prep. Time: 15 minutes ❧ Cooking Time: 3–4 hours ❧ Ideal slow-cooker size: 4-qt.

Needed at Time of Preparation:

1½ lbs. boneless, skinless chicken thighs

16-oz. jar salsa, as hot or mild as you like *choose a gluten-free brand to keep this recipe gluten-free

15-oz. can black beans

½ lb. fresh or frozen corn

1 Tbsp. chili powder

½ Tbsp. cumin

1 Tbsp. minced garlic

1 tsp. dried oregano

¼ tsp. cayenne pepper

¼ tsp. salt

freshly ground black pepper to taste

¼ cup water

Preparation Instructions:

1. Place all ingredients into a gallon-sized freezer bag.

2. Remove as much air as possible and seal bag.

3. Label the bag with the information below, then freeze.

TIP: If 8 servings is just too much for you, either split the recipe between 2 freezer bags or make it all and freeze the leftovers.

Information for Freezer Bag:

TACO CHICKEN BOWLS

Makes 8 servings

Cooking Time: 3–4 hours ❧ Ideal slow-cooker size: 4-qt.

Needed at Time of Serving:

2 cups uncooked rice

2 cups shredded cheese

cilantro, chopped

favorite salsa or hot sauce

Instructions:

1. Thaw bag completely for 24–48 hours or more.
2. Grease interior of slow-cooker crock.
3. Empty contents of freezer bag into crock and spread out evenly.
4. Cover. Cook on Low 3–4 hours, or until instant-read meat thermometer inserted into center of thigh registers 160–165°F.
5. Near end of chicken's cooking time, cook 2 cups of rice in microwave or stove top, according to its package directions.
6. When chicken is done cooking, stir with a fork to shred meat. Or using a slotted spoon, lift chicken into large bowl and shred it with 2 forks. Stir back into sauce and keep warm.
7. Have each diner make a pile of rice on her/his plate. Top with taco chicken mixture, then shredded cheese, fresh cilantro, and salsa or hot sauce.

Chicken Taco Salad

*5 Ing. or Fewer *Quick to Prep *Gluten-Free–Optional

Colleen Heatwole, Burton, MI

Makes 6 servings

Prep. Time: 30 minutes   ✽   Cooking Time: 4–6 hours   ✽   Ideal slow-cooker size: 4- to 5-qt.

Needed at Time of Preparation:

4 boneless, skinless chicken breasts

14½-oz. can diced tomatoes with green chiles *choose a gluten-free brand to keep this recipe gluten-free

1¼-oz. envelope taco seasoning mix *choose a gluten-free brand to keep this recipe gluten-free

Preparation Instructions:

1. Add all ingredients to a gallon-sized freezer bag. Massage bag well.

2. Remove as much air as possible and seal bag.

3. Label the bag with the information below, then freeze.

TIP: This recipe is so easy to assemble, you may want to consider doubling the ingredients and prepping 2 freezer-bag meals instead of just 1.

Instructions for Freezer Bag:

CHICKEN TACO SALAD

Makes 6 servings

Cooking Time: 4–6 hours   ✽   Ideal slow-cooker size: 4- to 5-qt.

Needed at Time of Serving:

Serve with usual desired taco salad condiments such as grated cheddar cheese, chopped tomato, chopped lettuce of choice, avocado, and tortilla chips.

Instructions:

1. Thaw bag completely (24–48 hours or more).

2. Place contents of freezer bag in crock and cook on Low 4–6 hours.

3. Cut chicken up into 2-inch pieces and return to sauce in crock while assembling other ingredients.

4. It is fun to serve "haystack" style with each diner adding ingredients of choice to the prepared taco chicken.

Magra's Chicken and Rice

*10 Ing. or Fewer *Gluten-Free

Carolyn Spohn, Shawnee, KS

Makes 8 servings

Prep. Time: 20 minutes   ❦   Cooking Time: 5 hours   ❦   Ideal slow-cooker size: 6-qt.

Needed at Time of Preparation:

2–3 medium carrots, chopped

1 medium onion, chopped

1 rib celery, chopped

2 cloves garlic, chopped

¼ tsp. dried rosemary, crumbled

3 cups chicken broth

8 boneless, skinless chicken thighs

Preparation Instructions:

1. Place all ingredients into a gallon-sized freezer bag.

2. Remove as much air as possible and seal bag.

3. Label the bag with the information below, then freeze.

TIP: If 8 servings is just too much for you, either split the recipe between 2 freezer bags or make it all and freeze the leftovers.

Information for Freezer Bag:

MAGRA'S CHICKEN AND RICE

Makes 8 servings

Cooking Time: 5 hours   ❦   Ideal slow-cooker size: 6-qt.

Needed at Time of Cooking:

1½ cups prepared rice

Instructions:

1. Thaw bag completely for 24–48 hours or more.

2. Grease interior of slow-cooker crock.

3. Empty contents of freezer bag into crock.

4. Cover. Cook on Low 4½ hours.

5. Lift thighs onto platter and cover. Stir rice into broth.

6. Return chicken to cooker, pushing pieces down in the broth as much as possible.

7. Cover. Cook 30 more minutes on Low, or until instant-read meat thermometer registers 160–165°F when stuck in the thighs.

8. To serve, place thighs in deep serving dish. Surround them with rice, vegetables, and broth.

Jambalaya

Gluten-Free–Optional

Hope Comerford, Clinton Township, MI

Makes 4–5 servings

Prep. Time: 20 minutes ❧ *Cooking Time: 8 hours* ❧ *Ideal slow-cooker size: 3-qt.*

Needed at Time of Preparation:

I lb. boneless, skinless chicken, chopped into 1-inch pieces

½ lb. andouille sausage *choose a gluten-free brand to keep this recipe gluten-free

I large onion, chopped

I green bell pepper, seeded and chopped

2 cups chopped okra

I rib celery, chopped

28-oz. can diced tomatoes

I cup chicken broth *make sure yours is gluten-free to keep this recipe gluten-free

2 tsp. dried oregano

2 tsp. Cajun seasoning *make sure the brand you choose is gluten-free to keep this recipe gluten-free

I tsp. salt

I tsp. hot sauce *make sure the brand you choose is gluten-free to keep this recipe gluten-free

2 bay leaves

½ tsp. thyme

Preparation Instructions:

1. Add all ingredients into a gallon-sized freezer bag.

2. Remove as much air as possible and seal bag.

3. Label the bag with the information below, then freeze.

TIP: Make 5-minute rice while the shrimp is cooking and everything will be ready to go all at the same time!

Information for Freezer Bag:

JAMBALAYA

Makes 4–5 servings

Cooking Time: 8 hours ❧ *Ideal slow-cooker size: 3-qt.*

Needed at Time of Cooking/ Serving:

1 lb. frozen peeled and cooked shrimp, thawed

4–5 servings of cooked rice

Instructions:

1. Thaw bag completely for 24–48 hours or more.

2. Empty the contents of the freezer bag into the crock.

3. Cover and cook on Low for 8 hours.

4. Right before you are ready to serve, add the shrimp and let cook an additional 5 minutes.

5. Serve over rice.

Beef Main Dishes

Marinated Chuck Roast

*10 Ing. or Fewer *Quick to Prep *Gluten-Free–Optional

Susan Nafziger, Canton, KS

Makes 7–8 servings

Prep. Time: 15 minutes   ❦   Cooking Time: 5–7 hours   ❦   Ideal slow-cooker size: oval 5-qt.

Needed at Time of Preparation:

1 cup olive oil

1 cup soy sauce *replace with tamari or liquid aminos if you're making this recipe gluten-free

¼ cup red wine vinegar

½ cup chopped onions

⅓ tsp. garlic powder

¼ tsp. ground ginger

½ tsp. black pepper (coarsely ground is best)

½ tsp. dry mustard

3–4-lb. boneless beef chuck roast

Preparation Instructions:

1. Mix all ingredients except the beef, either by whisking together in a bowl or whirring the mixture in a blender.

2. Place roast in a gallon-sized freezer bag and pour marinade over top.

3. Remove as much air as possible and seal bag.

4. Label the bag with the information below, then freeze.

TIP: If 7–8 servings is just too much for you, either split the recipe between 2 freezer bags or make it all and freeze the leftovers.

Information for Freezer Bag:

MARINATED CHUCK ROAST

Makes 7–8 servings

Cooking Time: 5–7 hours   ❦   Ideal slow-cooker size: oval 5-qt.

Instructions:

1. Thaw bag completely for 24–48 hours or more.

2. Grease interior of slow-cooker crock.

3. Empty contents of freezer bag into crock.

4. Cover. Cook on Low 5–6 hours, or until instant-read meat thermometer registers 140–145°F when stuck into center of meat.

5. When finished cooking, use a sturdy pair of tongs, or 2 metal spatulas, to move roast onto a cutting board. Cover to keep warm and allow to stand 15 minutes.

6. Cut into slices or chunks. Top with marinade and serve.

Pot Roast

*10 Ing. or Fewer *Gluten-Free–Optional*

Colleen Heatwole
Burton, MI

Makes 6 servings

Prep. Time: 20 minutes ❧ *Cooking Time: 6–8 hours* ❧ *Ideal slow-cooker size: 3- to 5-qt.*

Needed at Time of Preparation:

2½-lb. beef roast

2 Tbsp. steak sauce *make sure yours is gluten-free to keep this recipe gluten-free

1 medium onion, thinly sliced

6-oz. can tomato paste

1 cup ketchup

2 tsp. honey

¼ tsp. pepper

1 Tbsp. horseradish

Preparation Instructions:

1. In a gallon-sized freezer bag, place the beef roast and all the marinade ingredients in the order listed at left.

2. Seal the bag and massage or turn over several times until thoroughly mixed. Remove as much air as possible.

3. Label bag with the information below, then freeze.

Information for Freezer Bag:

POT ROAST

Makes 6 servings

Cooking Time: 6–8 hours ❧ *Ideal slow-cooker size: 3- to 5-qt.*

Needed at Time of Cooking:

potatoes and baby carrots, *optional*

Instructions:

1. Thaw bag completely for 24–48 hours or more

2. Empty contents of bag into crock. Add potatoes and baby carrots if desired.

3. Cover and cook 6–8 hours on Low.

Flavorful Pot Roast

*5 Ing. or Fewer *Quick to Prep*

Mary Kay Nolt, Newmanstown, PA

Makes 10–12 servings

Prep. Time: 10 minutes ❦ Cooking Time: 7–8 hours ❦ Ideal slow-cooker size: 5-qt.

Needed at Time of Preparation:

2 2½-lb. boneless beef chuck roasts

1 envelope dry ranch salad dressing mix

1 envelope dry Italian salad dressing mix

1 envelope dry brown gravy mix

½ cup water

Preparation Instructions:

1. Place all ingredients into a gallon-sized freezer bag and smoosh around.

2. Remove as much air as possible and seal bag.

3. Label with the information below, then freeze.

TIP: If 10–12 servings is just too much for you, either split the recipe between 2 freezer bags or make it all and freeze the leftovers.

Information for Freezer Bag:

FLAVORFUL POT ROAST

Makes 10–12 servings

Cooking Time: 7–8 hours ❦ Ideal slow-cooker size: 5-qt.

Needed at Time of Cooking:

1 Tbsp. flour plus ½ cup water, *optional*

Instructions:

1. Thaw bag completely for 24–48 hours or more.

2. Empty contents of freezer bag into crock.

3. Cover and cook on Low 7–8 hours, or until meat is tender but not dry.

4. Remove meat at end of cooking time and keep warm on a platter. If you wish, thicken the cooking juices for gravy with following steps.

5. Turn cooker to High. Bring juices to a boil.

6. Meanwhile, mix 1 Tbsp. flour with ½ cup water in a jar with a tight-fitting lid. Shake until smooth.

7. When juices come to a boil, pour flour/water mixture into cooker in a thin stream, stirring constantly. Continue cooking and stirring until juices thicken.

8. Serve gravy over meat or in a side dish along with the meat.

Herbed Pot Roast

*Gluten-Free

Sarah Herr, Goshen, IN

Makes 6 servings

Prep. Time: 20 minutes   ❧   Cooking Time: 6–8 hours   ❧   Ideal slow-cooker size: oval 6-qt.

Needed at Time of Preparation:

2-lb. boneless beef chuck roast

1 Tbsp. olive oil

3 carrots, peeled and cut into small chunks

2 ribs celery, cut into small chunks

½ tsp. salt

½ tsp. dried rosemary

½ tsp. dried thyme

¼ tsp. garlic powder

¼ tsp. onion powder

¼ tsp. paprika

¼ tsp. coarsely ground pepper

3 Tbsp. balsamic vinegar

Preparation Instructions:

1. Place all ingredients into a gallon-sized freezer bag. Smoosh around.

2. Remove as much air as possible and seal bag.

3. Label the bag with the information below, then freeze.

Information for Freezer Bag:

HERBED POT ROAST

Makes 6 servings

Cooking Time: 6–8 hours   ❧   Ideal slow-cooker size: oval 6-qt.

Needed at Time of Cooking:

3 medium potatoes, peeled or not, cut into small chunks

Instructions:

1. Thaw bag completely for 24–48 hours or more.

2. Grease interior of crock.

3. Place potatoes in bottom of crock, then empty contents of the freezer bag over the top.

4. Cover. Cook on Low 6–8 hours.

Green Chile Roast

*5 Ing. or Fewer *Quick to Prep *Gluten-Free–Optional

Anna Kenagy, Carlsbad, NM

Makes 8–10 servings

Prep. Time: 5 minutes ❧ Cooking Time: 8 hours ❧ Ideal slow-cooker size: 4-qt.

Needed at Time of Preparation:

3–4-lb. beef roast

olive oil, *optional*

I tsp. salt

3–4 green chiles, or 4-oz. can green chiles, undrained

I Tbsp. Worcestershire sauce
*make sure yours is gluten-free to keep recipe gluten-free

½ tsp. pepper

Preparation Instructions:

1. Add all ingredients to a gallon-sized freezer bag and smoosh around.

2. Remove as much air as possible and seal bag.

3. Label the bag with the information below, then freeze.

TIP: If 8–10 servings is just too much for you, either split the recipe between 2 freezer bags or make it all and freeze the leftovers.

Information for Freezer Bag:

GREEN CHILE ROAST

Makes 8–10 servings

Cooking Time: 8 hours ❧ Ideal slow-cooker size: 4-qt.

Instructions:

1. Thaw bag completely for 24–48 hours or more.

2. Empty contents of freezer bag into crock.

3. Cover. Cook on Low 8 hours.

BEEF ROAST WITH HOMEMADE GINGER-ORANGE SAUCE

Makes 8 servings

Cooking Time: 6–8 hours ⚘ *Ideal slow-cooker size: 7-qt.*

Serving Suggestion: Serve over mashed potatoes or rice. Or serve in sandwiches.

Instructions:

1. Thaw bag completely for 24–48 hours or more.

2. Grease interior of slow-cooker crock.

3. Empty roast from freezer bag #1 into crock.

4. Cover. Cook on Low 6–8 hours, or until an instant-read meat thermometer registers 150–160°F when stuck in center of roast.

5. About 45–50 minutes before the end of cooking time, empty contents of bag #2 in saucepan. Simmer 15 minutes, stirring occasionally so it doesn't stick.

6. Using sturdy tongs or 2 metal spatulas, lift cooked roast into big bowl. Shred with 2 forks.

7. Drain drippings and broth out of slow cooker. Save for gravy or soup.

8. Return shredded meat to crock. Stir in the sauce you made on the stove from bag #2.

9. Cover slow cooker again. Cook on Low 30 minutes, or until heated through.

Beef Roast with Homemade Ginger-Orange Sauce

*10 Ing. or Fewer *Gluten-Free–Optional*

Beverly Hummel, Fleetwood, PA

Makes 8 servings

Prep. Time: 20 minutes   ❧   Cooking Time: 6–8 hours   ❧   Ideal slow-cooker size: 7-qt.

Needed at Time of Preparation:

3-lb. boneless beef chuck roast

½ tsp. salt

¼ tsp. pepper

2 cups soy sauce *replace with tamari or liquid aminos to keep recipe gluten-free

½ cup brown sugar

½ cup white sugar

¼ cup minced onion

1 Tbsp. ground ginger

1 clove garlic, minced

½ cup orange juice

TIP: If 8 servings is just too much for you, either split the recipe between 2 freezer bags or make it all and freeze the leftovers.

Preparation instructions:

1. Salt and pepper the roast on all sides and seal in a freezer bag, removing as much air as possible. Label "#1."

2. In a second freezer bag, add the remaining ingredients. Remove as much air as possible and seal bag. Label "#2."

3. Place both bags into a third gallon-sized freezer bag and remove as much air as possible.

4. Label the third bag with the information opposite, then freeze.

Chuck Roast Beef Barbecue

*10 Ing. or Fewer *Gluten-Free–Optional

Helen Heurich, Lititz, PA

Makes 20 servings

Prep. Time: 30–40 minutes ❧ Cooking Time: 5–10 hours ❧ Ideal slow-cooker size: oval 6-qt.

Needed at Time of Preparation:

3-lb. boneless beef chuck roast

⅔ cup sriracha or barbecue sauce *make sure your choice is gluten-free to keep this recipe gluten-free

1¼ cups traditional tomato ketchup

3 Tbsp. lemon juice

2 Tbsp. Worcestershire sauce *make sure yours is gluten-free to keep this recipe gluten-free

2 Tbsp. brown sugar

1½ tsp. spicy brown prepared mustard *make sure yours is gluten-free to keep this recipe gluten-free

3 Tbsp. apple cider vinegar, *optional*

1–2 medium onions, chopped

3–4 ribs celery, chopped

Preparation Instructions:

1. Place all ingredients into a gallon-sized freezer bag and smoosh around.

2. Remove as much air as possible and seal bag.

3. Label the bag with the information below, then freeze.

TIP: If 20 servings is just too much for you, either split the recipe between 4 freezer bags or make it all and freeze the leftovers into portions appropriate for your family.

Information for Freezer Bag:

CHUCK ROAST BEEF BARBECUE

Makes 20 servings

Cooking Time: 5–10 hours ❧ Ideal slow-cooker size: oval 6-qt.

Needed at Time of Serving:

sandwich rolls

Instructions:

1. Thaw bag completely for 24–48 hours or more.

2. Grease interior of slow-cooker crock.

3. Empty contents of freezer bag into crock.

4. Cover. Cook on Low 8–10 hours, or on High 5–6 hours.

5. Using 2 forks, pull the meat apart until it's shredded. Do this in the cooker, or lift out the roast and do it on a good-sized cutting board or big bowl.

6. Return the shredded meat to the cooker and mix the sauce through it. Serve in toasted sandwich rolls.

Beef Chuck Barbecue

*10 Ing. or Fewer *Gluten-Free–Optional

Frances Kruba, Baltimore, MD

Makes 12 servings

Prep. Time: 10–15 minutes ⅋ Cooking Time: 6½–8½ hours ⅋ Ideal slow-cooker size: 5-qt.

Needed at Time of Preparation:

3-lb. boneless beef chuck roast, cut into quarters

1 cup of your favorite barbecue sauce *make sure yours is gluten-free to keep this recipe gluten-free

½ cup apricot jam

⅓ cup chopped green or red bell pepper

1 small onion, chopped

1 Tbsp. Dijon or your favorite spicy mustard *make sure yours is gluten-free to keep this recipe gluten-free

1 Tbsp. brown sugar

Preparation Instructions:

1. Place all ingredients into a gallon-sized freezer bag and smoosh around.

2. Remove as much air as possible and seal bag.

3. Label the bag with the information below, then freeze.

TIP: If 12 servings is just too much for you, either split the recipe between 2–3 freezer bags or make it all and freeze the leftovers into portions appropriate for your family.

Information for Freezer Bag:

BEEF CHUCK BARBECUE

Makes 12 servings

Cooking Time: 6½–8½ hours ⅋ Ideal slow-cooker size: 5-qt.

Needed at Time of Serving:

12 sandwich rolls

Instructions:

1. Thaw bag completely for 24–48 hours or more.

2. Grease interior of slow-cooker crock.

3. Empty contents of freezer bag into crock.

4. Cover. Cook on Low for 6–8 hours, or until meat is tender and instant-read meat thermometer registers 145°F when stuck in center of roast.

5. Remove roast from crock with sturdy tongs or 2 metal spatulas. Place on cutting board and slice thinly.

6. Return meat to crock and stir gently into sauce.

7. Cover. Cook 20–30 minutes longer on Low.

8. Serve beef and sauce on sandwich rolls.

Barbecued Brisket

Gluten-Free–Optional

Dorothy Dyer, Lee's Summit, MO

Makes 9–12 servings

Prep. Time: 15 minutes ❧ Cooking Time: 4–8 hours
Marinating Time: 12 hours ❧ Ideal slow-cooker size: oval 6-qt.

Needed at Time of Preparation:

3–4-lb. beef brisket

⅓ cup Italian salad dressing *make sure yours is gluten-free to keep this recipe gluten-free

1½ tsp. liquid smoke *make sure yours is gluten-free to keep this recipe gluten-free

⅓ cup + 2 tsp. brown sugar, packed

½ tsp. celery salt

½ tsp. salt

1 Tbsp. Worcestershire sauce *make sure yours is gluten-free to keep this recipe gluten-free

½ tsp. black pepper (coarsely ground is best)

¼ tsp. chili powder

½ tsp. garlic powder

1¼ cups barbecue sauce *make sure yours is gluten-free to keep this recipe gluten-free

Preparation Instructions:

1. Place all ingredients into a gallon-sized freezer bag and smoosh around.

2. Remove as much air as possible and seal bag.

3. Label the bag with the information below, then freeze.

TIP: If 9–12 servings is just too much for you, either split the recipe between 3–4 freezer bags or make it all and freeze the leftovers into portions appropriate for your family.

Information for Freezer Bag:

BARBECUED BRISKET

Makes 9–12 servings

Cooking Time: 4–8 hours ❧ Ideal slow-cooker size: oval 6-qt.

Instructions:

1. Thaw bag completely for 24–48 hours or more.

2. Grease interior of slow-cooker crock.

3. Empty contents of freezer bag into crock.

4. Cover. Cook on Low for 6–8 hours, or on High 4–5 hours, or until instant-read meat thermometer registers 140–145°F when stuck in center of meat.

5. Using sturdy tongs or 2 metal spatulas, lift meat onto cutting board. Cover with foil to keep warm. Let stand 20 minutes.

6. Slice diagonally, across grain, into ½-inch-thick slices. Place slices in long baking dish.

7. Pour barbecue sauce over sliced meat. Broil for 5 minutes or so, to brown. Watch carefully so it doesn't burn.

Shredded BBQ Brisket

*10 Ing. or Fewer *Quick to Prep *Gluten-Free–Optional

Amanda Gross, Souderton, PA

Makes 6–8 servings

Prep. Time: 5 minutes ❦ Cooking Time: 9–10 hours ❦ Ideal slow-cooker size: 7-qt.

Needed at Time of Preparation:

3–4-lb. beef brisket

18 oz. barbecue sauce *make sure yours is gluten-free to keep this recipe gluten-free

2 tsp. chili powder

2 tsp. garlic powder

1 tsp. cumin

1 tsp. onion powder

½ tsp. salt

½ tsp. pepper

Preparation Instructions:

1. Place all ingredients into a gallon-sized freezer bag and massage around all ingredients.

2. Remove as much air as possible and seal bag.

3. Label the bag with the information below, then freeze.

TIP: If 6–8 servings is just too much for you, either split the recipe between 2 freezer bags or make it all and freeze the leftovers.

Information for Freezer Bag:

SHREDDED BBQ BRISKET

Makes 6–8 servings

Cooking Time: 9–10 hours ❦ Ideal slow-cooker size: 7-qt.

Needed at Time of Serving:

9–10 brioche buns *replace with gluten-free buns if you're making this gluten-free

Instructions:

1. Thaw bag completely for 24–48 hours or more.

2. Place all ingredients from freezer bag in crock.

3. Cover and cook on Low 9–10 hours.

4. Remove meat from crock, shred with a fork, then stir the shredded meat back through the sauce in the crock.

5. Serve on brioche buns.

Brisket with Tomatoes and Sauerkraut

*5 Ing. or Fewer *Quick to Prep *Gluten-Free–Optional

Alyce C. Kauffman, Gridley, CA

Makes 6–8 servings

Prep. Time: 15 minutes   ❦   Cooking Time: 4–7 hours   ❦   Ideal slow-cooker size: 5-qt.

Needed at Time of Preparation:

15½-oz. can stewed tomatoes, cut up and undrained

8-oz. can sauerkraut, undrained *make sure yours is gluten-free to keep this recipe gluten-free

1 cup applesauce

2 Tbsp. brown sugar

2½–3½-lb. beef brisket

Preparation instructions:

1. Place all ingredients into a gallon-sized freezer bag and smoosh around.

2. Remove as much air as possible and seal bag.

3. Label the bag with the information below, then freeze.

TIP: If 6–8 servings is just too much for you, either split the recipe between 2 freezer bags or make it all and freeze the leftovers.

Information for Freezer Bag:

BRISKET WITH TOMATOES AND SAUERKRAUT

Makes 6–8 servings

Cooking Time: 4–7 hours   ❦   Ideal slow-cooker size: 5-qt.

Needed at Time of Cooking/Serving:

2 Tbsp. cold water

2 Tbsp. cornstarch

sprigs of fresh parsley

Instructions:

1. Thaw bag completely for 24–48 hours or more.

2. Grease interior of slow-cooker crock.

3. Empty contents of freezer bag into crock.

4. Cover. Cook on Low 6–7 hours, or on High 4–5 hours, or until instant-read meat thermometer registers 140–145°F when stuck in center of meat.

5. Uncover and lift brisket onto cutting board using sturdy tongs or 2 metal spatulas. Cover to keep warm. Let stand 15 minutes.

6. Meanwhile, turn cooker to High. Combine cold water and cornstarch until smooth. Stir into sauce in crock. Continue stirring until sauce thickens and bubbles.

7. Cut brisket into chunks or slices. Spoon some of the sauce over the meat. Serve remaining sauce as gravy.

8. Just before serving, garnish meat with parsley.

Beef Burgundy with Mushrooms

*10 Ing. or Fewer *Gluten-Free

Rosemarie Fitzgerald, Gibsonia, PA

Makes 6 servings

Prep. Time: 15 minutes ❦ Cooking Time: 5¼–6¼ hours ❦ Ideal slow-cooker size: 5-qt.

Needed at Time of Preparation:

2–3-lb. boneless beef chuck roast, cut into 1½-inch pieces

1 cup chopped onions

2 cloves garlic

2 cups burgundy

¼–½ tsp. marjoram, according to your taste preference

½ lb. fresh mushrooms, sliced, or canned and drained

Preparation Instructions:

1. Place all ingredients into a gallon-sized freezer bag and smoosh around.

2. Remove as much air as possible and seal bag.

3. Label the bag with the information below, then freeze.

TIP: This recipe is so easy to assemble, you may want to consider doubling the ingredients now and prepping 2 freezer-bag meals instead of just 1.

Information for Freezer Bag:

BEEF BURGUNDY WITH MUSHROOMS

Makes 6 servings

Cooking Time: 5¼–6¼ hours ❦ Ideal slow-cooker size: 5-qt.

Needed at Time of Cooking:

6-oz. can tomato paste

dash sugar

Serving Suggestion: Serve over cooked noodles, rice, or potatoes.

Instructions:

1. Thaw bag completely for 24–48 hours or more.

2. Grease interior of slow-cooker crock.

3. Empty contents of freezer bag into crock.

4. Cover and cook on Low 4½–5½ hours.

5. Cover and continue cooking 30 more minutes.

6. Stir in tomato paste and sugar. Cook another 10–15 minutes, uncovered, to allow sauce to thicken.

Hungarian Beef with Paprika

*10 Ing. or Fewer *Gluten-Free

Maureen Csikasz, Wakefield, MA

Makes 9 servings

Prep. Time: 15 minutes ❧ *Cooking Time: 3–6 hours* ❧ *Ideal slow-cooker size: oval 5- or 6-qt.*

Needed at Time of Preparation:

3-lb. boneless beef chuck roast

2–3 medium onions, coarsely chopped

5 Tbsp. sweet paprika

¾ tsp. salt

¼ tsp. black pepper

½ tsp. caraway seeds

1 clove garlic, chopped

½ green bell pepper, sliced

¼ cup water

Preparation Instructions:

1. Place all ingredients into a gallon-sized freezer bag and smoosh around.

2. Remove as much air as possible and seal bag.

3. Label the bag with the information below, then freeze.

TIP: If 9 servings is just too much for you, either split the recipe between 2 freezer bags or make it all and freeze the leftovers.

Information for Freezer Bag:

HUNGARIAN BEEF WITH PAPRIKA

Makes 9 servings

Cooking Time: 3–6 hours ❧ *Ideal slow-cooker size: oval 5- or 6-qt.*

Needed at Time of Serving:

½ cup sour cream, *optional*

fresh parsley

Serving Suggestion: Serve with buttered noodles or potatoes.

Instructions:

1. Thaw bag completely for 24–48 hours or more.

2. Grease interior of slow-cooker crock.

3. Empty contents of freezer bag into crock.

4. Cover. Cook on High 3–4 hours, or on Low 5–6 hours, or until instant-read meat thermometer registers 140–145°F when stuck in center of meat.

5. When finished cooking, use sturdy tongs or 2 metal spatulas to lift meat to cutting board. Cover with foil to keep warm. Let stand 10–15 minutes.

6. Cut into chunks or slices.

7. Just before serving, dollop with the sour cream, if using. Garnish with fresh parsley.

Four-Pepper Steak

Gluten-Free

Renee Hankins, Narvon, PA

Makes 14 servings

Prep. Time: 30 minutes ❦ Cooking Time: 5–8 hours ❦ Ideal slow-cooker size: 4- or 5-qt.

Needed at Time of Preparation:

1 yellow pepper, sliced into ¼-inch-thick pieces

1 red pepper, sliced into ¼-inch-thick pieces

1 orange pepper, sliced into ¼-inch-thick pieces

1 green pepper, sliced into ¼-inch-thick pieces

2 cloves garlic, sliced

2 large onions, sliced

1 tsp. ground cumin

½ tsp. dried oregano

1 bay leaf

3-lb. flank steak, cut in ¼–½-inch-thick slices across the grain

salt to taste

2 14½-oz. cans low-sodium diced tomatoes in juice

jalapeño chiles, sliced, *optional*

Preparation Instructions:

1. Place all ingredients into a gallon-sized freezer bag and smoosh together.

2. Remove as much air as possible and seal bag.

3. Label the bag with the information below, then freeze.

TIP: If 14 servings is just too much for you, either split the recipe between 3–4 freezer bags or make it all and freeze the leftovers into portions appropriate for your family.

Information for Freezer Bag:

FOUR-PEPPER STEAK

Makes 14 servings

Cooking Time: 5–8 hours ❦ Ideal slow-cooker size: 4- or 5-qt.

Instructions:

1. Thaw bag completely for 24–48 hours.

2. Empty contents of freezer bag into crock.

3. Cover and cook on Low 5–8 hours, depending on your slow cooker. Check after 5 hours to see if meat is tender. If not, continue cooking until tender but not dry. Remove bay leaf and serve.

Marinated Flank Steak with Broccoli

*10 Ing. or Fewer *Gluten-Free–Optional

Amanda Gross, Souderton, PA

Makes 4–6 servings

Prep. Time: 5–10 minutes 🌱 Cooking Time: 3–4 hours 🌱 Ideal slow-cooker size: 7-qt.

Needed at Time of Preparation:

2-lb. flank steak, sliced into thin strips

2 cups beef broth *make sure yours is gluten-free to keep this recipe gluten-free

½ cup soy sauce *replace with tamari or liquid aminos if you're making this recipe gluten-free

¼ cup brown sugar

2 cloves garlic, minced

1 Tbsp. sesame oil

2 cups broccoli florets

Preparation Instructions:

1. Place all ingredients into a gallon-sized freezer bag and massage to combine all ingredients.

2. Remove as much air as possible and seal bag.

3. Label the bag with the information below, then freeze.

Information for Freezer Bag:

MARINATED FLANK STEAK WITH BROCCOLI

Makes 4–6 servings

Cooking Time: 3–4 hours 🌱 Ideal slow-cooker size: 7-qt.

Needed at Time of Serving:

Cooked rice

Instructions:

1. Thaw bag completely for 24–48 hours or more.

2. Add everything from freezer bag to crock.

3. Cover and cook on High 3–4 hours.

4. Serve with rice.

Italian Cheesesteak Sandwiches

*10 Ing. or Fewer *Quick to Prep *Gluten-Free–Optional

Jennifer Archer, Kalona, IA

Makes 8–10 servings

Prep. Time: 10 minutes ❦ Cooking Time: 10–12 hours ❦ Ideal slow-cooker size: 6-qt.

Needed at Time of Preparation:

3-lb. boneless beef chuck roast

1 envelope dry Italian dressing mix *make sure yours is gluten-free to keep this recipe gluten-free

2–3 bay leaves

1 Tbsp. dried basil

1 Tbsp. dried oregano

2–3 tsp. garlic powder, according to taste

1–2 cups beef broth *make sure yours is gluten-free to keep this recipe gluten-free

¼–½ tsp. coarsely ground black pepper, according to taste

Preparation Instructions:

1. Place all ingredients into a gallon-sized freezer bag and smoosh all of the ingredients together.

2. Remove as much air as possible and seal bag.

3. Label the bag with the information below, then freeze.

TIP: If 8–10 servings is just too much for you, either split the recipe between 2 freezer bags or make it all and freeze the leftovers into portions appropriate for your family.

Information for Freezer Bag:

ITALIAN CHEESESTEAK SANDWICHES

Makes 8–10 servings

Cooking Time: 10–12 hours ❦ Ideal slow-cooker size: 6-qt.

Needed at Time of Serving:

8–10 steak rolls *replace with gluten-free rolls to make this recipe gluten-free

8–10 slices provolone or mozzarella cheese

Instructions:

1. Thaw bag completely for 24–48 hours or more.
2. Grease interior of slow-cooker crock.
3. Empty contents of freezer bag into crock.
4. Cover. Cook 6–8 hours on Low, or until instant-read meat thermometer registers 145–150°F when stuck in center of roast.
5. Lift roast out of crock with 2 sturdy metal spatulas onto cutting board. Use 2 forks to shred. Fish out bay leaves.
6. Return shredded meat to crock and stir into sauce.
7. Place rolls open-faced on baking sheet. Using a slotted spoon, pile each roll with beef and slice of cheese. Place under broiler for 2–3 minutes, until cheese is bubbly.

Beef and Pepperoncini Hoagies

*5 Ing. or Fewer *Quick to Prep *Gluten-Free

Donna Treloar, Muncie, IN

Makes 10 servings

Prep. Time: 15 minutes ❦ Cooking Time: 8–10 hours ❦ Ideal slow-cooker size: 5- or 6-qt.

Needed at Time of Preparation:

4-lb. boneless beef chuck roast

16-oz. jar of pepperoncini peppers, mild or medium, depending on your preference, stems removed

1 clove garlic, minced, or 1 tsp. garlic powder

salt and pepper, to taste

Preparation Instructions:

1. Place all ingredients into a gallon-sized freezer bag.

2. Remove as much air as possible and seal bag.

3. Label the bag with the information below, then freeze.

TIP: If 10 servings is just too much for you, either split the recipe between 2 freezer bags or make it all and freeze the leftovers into portions appropriate for your family.

Information for Freezer Bag:

BEEF AND PEPPERONCINI HOAGIES

Makes 10 servings

Cooking Time: 8–10 hours ❦ Ideal slow-cooker size: 5- or 6-qt.

Needed at Time of Serving:

hoagie rolls or buns of your choice *replace with gluten-free buns to keep this recipe gluten-free

20 slices provolone cheese

Instructions:

1. Thaw bag completely for 24–48 hours or more.
2. Grease interior of slow-cooker crock.
3. Empty contents of freezer bag into crock.
4. Cover. Cook on Low 7½–9½ hours, or until beef registers 160°F on an instant-read meat thermometer when stuck in center of roast.
5. Lift roast into a big bowl and shred with 2 forks.
6. Stir shredded meat back into juices in crock.
7. Cover. Cook another 30 minutes on Low.
8. When ready to serve, use a slotted spoon to drain meat well.
9. Spoon well-drained meat onto a hoagie roll and top each sandwich with 2 slices cheese.

Italian Beef Sandwiches

*5 Ing. or Fewer *Quick to Prep *Gluten-Free*

Hope Comerford, Clinton Township, MI

Makes 6–8 servings

Prep. Time: 5 minutes   ❦   Cooking Time: 8–10 hours   ❦   Ideal slow-cooker size: 3-qt.

Needed at Time of Preparation:

3½–4½-lb. English roast

16-oz. jar pepperoncini

Preparation Instructions:

1. Place all ingredients into a gallon-sized freezer bag.

2. Remove as much air as possible and seal bag.

3. Label the bag with the information below, then freeze.

TIP: If 6–8 servings is just too much for you, either split the recipe between 2 freezer bags or make it all and freeze the leftovers.

Information for Freezer Bag:

ITALIAN BEEF SANDWICHES

Makes 6–8 servings

Cooking Time: 8–10 hours   ❦   Ideal slow-cooker size: 3-qt.

Needed at Time of Serving:

6–8 sub buns *choose gluten-free buns to keep this recipe gluten-free

butter

6–8 large slices provolone or mozzarella cheese

Instructions:

1. Thaw bag completely for 24-48 hours or more.

2. Empty contents of freezer bag into crock.

3. Cover and cook on Low for 8–10 hours.

4. Remove the roast and shred it between two forks. Replace it back into the crock and stir it through the juices.

5. Preheat the oven to 400°F.

6. Place each sub bun open-faced on a foil-lined cookie sheet. Spread a bit of butter on each side. Place the cheese on top of each bun. Place them in the oven for about 8 minutes, or until the bread is slightly toasted and the cheese is melted.

7. Remove the sub buns from the oven and place a good portion of Italian beef on top.

Fabulous Fajitas

*10 Ing. or Fewer *Gluten-Free–Optional

Phyllis Good, Lancaster, PA

Makes 4 servings

Prep. Time: 15 minutes ❦ Cooking Time: 3½ hours ❦ Ideal slow-cooker size: 4-qt.

Needed at Time of Preparation:

1–1½ lbs. flank steak, cut across grain in ½-inch-thick strips

2 Tbsp. lemon juice

1 clove garlic, minced

1½ tsp. cumin

½ tsp. red pepper flakes

1 tsp. seasoning salt

2 Tbsp. Worcestershire sauce *make sure yours is gluten-free to keep this recipe gluten-free

1 tsp. chili powder

Preparation Instructions:

1. Place all ingredients inside a gallon-sized freezer bag and smoosh around to coat everything evenly.

2. Remove as much air as possible and seal bag.

3. Label the bag with the information below, then freeze.

Information for Freezer Bag:

FABULOUS FAJITAS

Makes 4 servings

Cooking Time: 3½ hours ❦ Ideal slow-cooker size: 4-qt.

Needed at Time of Cooking/Serving:

1 green bell pepper, cut in strips

1 yellow onion, sliced

6–8 warmed tortillas *use gluten-free tortillas to keep this recipe gluten-free

Sour cream, chopped fresh cilantro, salsa, shredded cheese, etc., *optional*

Instructions:

1. Thaw bag completely for 24–48 hours or more.

2. Grease interior of slow-cooker crock.

3. Empty contents of freezer bag into crock.

4. Cover and cook on Low 2½ hours, or until beef is nearly tender.

5. Stir in pepper and onion.

6. Cover. Cook for another hour on Low or until vegetables are as tender as you like them.

7. Spoon mixture into warm tortillas. Top with favorite toppings.

Fajita Steak

*5 Ing. or Fewer *Quick to Prep *Gluten-Free–Optional*

Becky Harder, Monument, CO

Makes 6 servings

Prep. Time: 10 minutes ❧ Cooking Time: 6–8 hours ❧ Ideal slow-cooker size: 4-qt.

Needed at Time of Preparation

15-oz. can diced tomatoes with green chiles

¼ cup salsa, your choice of mild, medium, or hot *be sure you choose a gluten-free brand to keep this recipe gluten-free

8-oz. can tomato sauce

2 lbs. round steak, cut in 2x4-inch strips

1 envelope dry fajita spice mix *be sure to choose a gluten-free brand to keep this recipe gluten-free

Preparation Instructions:

1. Place all ingredients in a gallon-sized freezer bag and smoosh everything together.

2. Remove as much air as possible and seal bag.

3. Label the bag with the information below, then freeze.

TIP: This recipe is so easy to assemble, you may consider doubling the ingredients now and prepping 2 freezer-bag meals instead of just 1.

Information for Freezer Bag:

FAJITA STEAK

Makes 6 servings

Cooking Time: 6–8 hours ❧ Ideal slow-cooker size: 4-qt.

Needed at Time of Cooking:

1 cup water, *optional*

Serving Suggestion: Serve meat with fried onions and green peppers. Offer shredded cheese, avocado chunks, and sour cream as toppings. Let individual eaters wrap any or all of the ingredients in flour tortillas.

Instructions:

1. Thaw bag completely for 24–48 hours or more.

2. Empty contents of freezer bag into crock.

3. Cover and cook on Low 6–8 hours, or until meat is tender but not overcooked.

4. Check meat occasionally to make sure it isn't cooking dry. If it begins to look dry, stir in water, up to 1 cup.

TOSTADAS

Makes 8–10 servings

Cooking Time: 6–8 hours ❦ *Ideal slow-cooker size: 5-qt.*

Needed at Time of Cooking/Serving:

1 Tbsp. lime juice

hard or soft tortillas *choose gluten-free tortillas to keep this recipe gluten-free

refried beans, cooked onions and bell peppers, chopped lettuce, shredded Mexican-blend cheese, salsa, guacamole, sour cream, *optional*

Instructions:

1. Thaw bag completely for 24–48 hours or more.

2. Grease interior of slow-cooker crock.

3. Empty contents of freezer bag into crock.

4. Cover. Cook on Low for 6–8 hours, or until instant-read meat thermometer registers 145–150°F when stuck in center of roast.

5. Remove beef to a cutting board and when cool enough to handle, shred with fingers or 2 forks.

6. Place shredded beef in large bowl. Strain remaining liquid in slow cooker over bowl or measuring cup, discarding solids.

7. Add strained liquid and add 1 Tbsp. lime juice to beef in bowl. Stir to combine.

8. Cover and keep warm until ready to serve in either hard or soft tortillas, along with your optional favorite toppings.

Tostadas

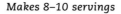

*10 Ing. or Fewer *Gluten-Free

Jenny Unternahrer, Wayland, IA

Makes 8–10 servings

Prep. Time: 15 minutes ❧ Cooking Time: 6–8 hours ❧ Ideal slow-cooker size: 5-qt.

Needed at Time of Preparation:

3 Tbsp. lime juice

3 cloves garlic, finely chopped

1 jalapeño, seeded and finely chopped

1 large onion, chopped

1 Tbsp. chili powder, or a combination of cumin, garlic powder, onion powder, and cayenne pepper

¼ tsp. cumin

⅛ tsp. cayenne pepper

1½ lbs. boneless beef chuck roast

½ tsp. salt

½ tsp. coarsely ground black pepper

Preparation Instructions:

1. Place all ingredients into a gallon-sized freezer bag and smoosh everything together.

2. Remove as much air as possible and seal bag.

3. Label the bag with the information opposite, then freeze.

TIP: If 8–10 servings is just too much for you, either split the recipe between 2 freezer bags or make it all and freeze the leftovers into portions appropriate for your family.

Saucy Tacos

*5 Ing. or Fewer *Quick to Prep *Gluten-Free–Optional

Sarah Herr, Goshen, IN

Makes 8 servings

Prep. Time: 10 minutes   ❦   Cooking Time: 6–8 hours   ❦   Ideal slow-cooker size: 4-qt.

Needed at Time of Preparation:

2 lbs. flank steak

1 green bell pepper, chopped

1 onion, chopped

1 cup salsa *choose a gluten-free brand to keep this recipe gluten-free

2 Tbsp., or 1 envelope, taco seasoning *choose a gluten-free brand to keep this recipe gluten-free

Preparation Instructions:

1. Place all ingredients into a gallon-sized freezer bag and smoosh around to coat everything.

2. Remove as much air as possible and seal bag.

3. Label the bag with the information below, then freeze.

TIP: If 8 servings is just too much for you, either split the recipe between 2 freezer bags or make it all and freeze the leftovers.

Information for Freezer Bag:

SAUCY TACOS

Makes 8 servings

Cooking Time: 6–8 hours   ❦   Ideal slow-cooker size: 4-qt.

Needed at Time of Serving:

tortillas or taco shells *choose gluten-free tortillas or taco shells to keep this recipe gluten-free

Instructions:

1. Thaw bag completely for 24–48 hours or more.

2. Grease interior of slow-cooker crock.

3. Empty contents of freezer bag into crock.

4. Cover. Cook 6–8 hours on Low, or until instant-read meat thermometer registers 140–145°F when stuck in center.

5. Shred meat with 2 forks, or slice thinly. Mix with vegetables and juice. Serve with tortillas or taco shells.

Beef Goulash

*10 Ing. or Fewer *Gluten-Free–Optional

Colleen Heatwole, Burton, MI

Makes 6 servings

Prep. Time: 30 minutes   ❦   Cooking Time: 8 hours   ❦   Ideal slow-cooker size: 4- to 5-qt.

Needed at Time of Preparation:

2 lbs. beef stew meat,
cut into bite-sized pieces

2 cups chopped onions

1 cup chopped carrots

1 medium red bell pepper, chopped
(about 1 cup)

¼ cup ketchup

2 tsp. Worcestershire sauce *choose a
gluten-free brand to keep this recipe
gluten-free

2 tsp. paprika

2 tsp. minced garlic

1 tsp. salt

16 oz. beef broth, low sodium
preferred *choose a gluten-free brand
to keep this recipe gluten-free

Preparation Instructions:

1. Place all ingredients into a gallon-sized freezer bag and smoosh around until everything is coated well.

2. Remove as much air as possible, then seal bag.

3. Label the bag with the information below, then freeze.

Information for Freezer Bag:

BEEF GOULASH

Makes 6 servings

Cooking Time: 8 hours   ❦   Ideal slow-cooker size: 4- to 5-qt.

Serving Suggestion: Mashed potatoes and green beans go well as sides.

Instructions:

1. Thaw bag completely for 24–48 hours or more.

2. Place contents of freezer bag in slow cooker.

3. Cover and cook on Low 8 hours.

4. Serve with sides of choice.

Stuffed Peppers

Mary Stoltzfus, Manheim, PA

Makes 6–8 servings

Prep. Time: 25 minutes ❦ *Cooking Time: 4–6 hours* ❦ *Ideal slow-cooker size: 6-qt.*

Needed at Time of Preparation:

2 lbs. ground beef

2 eggs

¾ cup rolled oats

½ cup barbecue sauce

⅓ cup milk

1 Tbsp. Worcestershire sauce

1 medium onion, chopped

scant 1¾ tsp. salt

scant ¾ tsp. dry mustard

½ tsp. black pepper

½ tsp. sage

1 clove garlic, minced

6–8 green peppers

Preparation Instructions:

1. Combine all ingredients except green peppers in a bowl.

2. Remove tops and inner membranes of peppers.

3. Fill peppers with meat filling.

4. Place stuffed peppers in freezer bag(s).

5. Remove as much air as possible and seal bag(s).

6. Label the bag(s) with the information below, then freeze.

TIP: If 6–8 servings is just too much for you, either split the recipe between 2 freezer bags or make it all and freeze the leftovers.

Information for Freezer Bag:

STUFFED PEPPERS

Makes 6–8 servings

Cooking Time: 4–6 hours ❦ *Ideal slow-cooker size: 6-qt.*

Needed at Time of Cooking/ Serving:

11¾-oz. can condensed cream of tomato soup

Cooked brown rice

Directions:

1. Thaw bag completely for 24–48 hours or more.

2. Stand filled peppers upright in crock.

3. Top with undiluted cream of tomato soup.

4. Cover and cook 4–6 hours on Low, or until peppers are soft and meat is cooked through.

5. Prepare desired amount of rice according to directions.

6. Serve peppers over rice.

Meatloaf

*10 Ing. or Fewer *Gluten-Free–Optional

Colleen Heatwole, Burton, MI

Makes 6–8 servings

Prep. Time: 15 minutes ❦ *Cooking Time: 4–6 hours* ❦ *Ideal slow-cooker size: 6-qt.*

Needed at Time of Preparation:

2 lbs. ground beef

2 eggs

2⁄3 cup dry quick oats *be sure to choose gluten-free oats to keep this recipe gluten-free

½ envelope of dry onion soup mix *choose a gluten-free brand to keep this recipe gluten-free

½–1 tsp. liquid smoke *choose a gluten-free brand to keep this recipe gluten-free

1 tsp. ground mustard

¼ cup plus 2 Tbsp. ketchup

Preparation instructions:

1. Add all ingredients into a gallon-sized freezer bag. Smoosh everything around until well-combined.

2. Remove as much air as possible and seal bag.

3. Label the bag with the information below, then freeze.

TIP: Leftover meatloaf makes great sandwiches! Or, freeze your leftover meatloaf slices into single portions for another day.

Information for Freezer Bag:

MEATLOAF

Makes 6–8 servings

Cooking Time: 4–6 hours ❦ *Ideal slow-cooker size: 6-qt.*

Needed at Time of Cooking:

2 Tbsp. ketchup

Serving Suggestion: Goes well with mashed potatoes and green beans.

Instructions:

1. Thaw bag completely for 24–48 hours or more.

2. Spray inside of slow cooker with cooking spray.

3. Shape contents of bag into a loaf and add to slow cooker.

4. Top with 2 Tbsp. ketchup.

5. Cover and cook on Low 4–6 hours or until instant-read thermometer registers 160°F when inserted into center of meatloaf.

Mexican Meatloaf

*10 Ing. or Fewer

Jennifer Freed, Rockingham, VA

Makes 4–6 servings

Prep. Time: 20 minutes   ❧   Cooking Time: 5–7 hours   ❧   Ideal slow-cooker size: 3- to 4-qt.

Needed at Time of Preparation:

2 lbs. ground beef

2 cups crushed saltines

1 cup shredded cheddar cheese

2/3 cup salsa

2 eggs, beaten

4 Tbsp. taco seasoning

Preparation Instructions:

1. Place all ingredients into a gallon-sized freezer bag and smoosh around until all ingredients are well-combined.

2. Remove as much air as possible and seal bag.

3. Label the bag with the information below, then freeze.

TIP: Leftover meatloaf makes great sandwiches! Or, freeze your leftover meatloaf slices into single portions for another day.

Information for Freezer Bag:

MEXICAN MEATLOAF

Makes 4–6 servings

Cooking Time: 5–7 hours   ❧   Ideal slow-cooker size: 3- to 4-qt.

Needed at Time of Cooking:

½ cup ketchup

2 Tbsp. brown sugar

1 tsp. dry mustard

Serving Suggestion: Goes well with corn and potato wedges.

Instructions:

1. Thaw bag completely for 24–48 hours or more.

2. Spray crock with nonstick spray.

3. Shape meat mixture from freezer bag into a loaf and place in slow cooker.

4. Cover and cook on Low for 5–7 hours, or until internal temperature is 165°F.

5. Mix together the ketchup, brown sugar and dry mustard. Spread over meatloaf. Cover and cook on High 15 minutes.

CHEESY BEEF AND PORK MEATLOAF

Makes 8 servings

Cooking Time: 4–5 hours ❧ *Ideal slow-cooker size: 5-qt.*

Serving Suggestion: Goes well with mashed potatoes and peas.

Instructions:

1. Thaw bag completely for 24–48 hours or more.

2. Grease interior of slow-cooker crock.

3. Make a tinfoil sling for your slow cooker so you can lift the cooked meatloaf out easily. Begin by folding a strip of foil accordion-fashion so that it's about 1½–2 inches wide, and long enough to fit from the top edge of the crock, down inside and up the other side, plus a 2-inch overhang on each side of the cooker. Make a second strip exactly like the first.

4. Place the one strip in the crock, running from end to end. Place the second strip in the crock, running from side to side. The 2 strips should form a cross in the bottom of the crock.

5. Remove contents of freezer bag, shape into a loaf, and place it in the crock, centering it where the 2 foil handles cross.

6. Cover. Cook on Low 4–5 hours, or until meatloaf is cooked in the center.

7. Using the foil handles, lift the meatloaf out of the crock and onto a cutting board. Allow to stand 15 minutes.

8. Cut into slices and serve.

Cheesy Beef and Pork Meatloaf

*Gluten-Free–Optional

Jean Turner, Williams Lake, BC

Makes 8 servings

Prep. Time: 15–20 minutes ❧ Cooking Time: 4–5 hours ❧ Ideal slow-cooker size: 5-qt.

Needed at Time of Preparation:

½ cup onions, chopped

½ cup green bell pepper, chopped

8-oz. can tomato sauce

2 eggs, beaten

1 cup white cheddar cheese, shredded

1 cup soft bread crumbs *choose gluten-free bread crumbs to keep this recipe gluten-free

1 tsp. salt

dash black pepper

¼ tsp. dried thyme

1½ lbs. ground beef

½ lb. ground pork

Preparation Instructions:

1. Place all ingredients into a gallon-sized freezer bag and smoosh until everything is well-combined.

2. Remove as much air as possible and seal bag.

3. Label the bag with the information opposite, then freeze.

TIP: Leftover meatloaf makes great sandwiches! Or, freeze your leftover meatloaf slices into single portions for another day.

MEATLOAF WITH SWEET TOMATO GLAZE

Makes 6–8 servings

Cooking Time: 4 hours ❦ *Ideal slow-cooker size: oval 5-qt.*

Needed at Time of Cooking:

3 Tbsp. brown sugar

¼ cup ketchup

1 tsp. dry mustard

Instructions:

1. Thaw bag completely for 24–48 hours or more.

2. Grease interior of slow-cooker crock.

3. Make a tinfoil sling for your slow cooker so you can lift the cooked meatloaf out easily. Begin by folding a strip of foil accordion-fashion so that it's about 1½–2 inches wide, and long enough to fit from the top edge of the crock, down inside and up the other side, plus a 2-inch overhang on each side of the cooker. Make a second strip exactly like the first.

4. Place the one strip in the crock, running from end to end. Place the second strip in the crock, running from side to side. The 2 strips should form a cross in the bottom of the crock.

5. Remove contents of freezer bag, shape into a loaf, and place it in the crock, centering it where the 2 foil handles cross.

6. In a bowl, mix the brown sugar, ketchup, and dry mustard together.

7. Spoon half the glaze over the meatloaf. Reserve the rest for later.

8. Cover. Cook on Low 4–5 hours.

9. Using the foil handles, lift meatloaf out of cooker. Place on rimmed baking sheet.

10. Spoon remaining glaze over top.

11. Place meat on rimmed baking sheet under broiler for 2–4 minutes. Keep watch so it browns and bubbles but doesn't burn.

12. Let stand for 10 minutes. Then slice and serve.

Meatloaf with Sweet Tomato Glaze

*10 Ing. or Fewer *Gluten-Free–Optional

Phyllis Good, Lancaster, PA

Makes 6–8 servings

Prep. Time: 15–20 minutes ❦ *Cooking Time: 4 hours* ❦ *Ideal slow-cooker size: oval 5-qt.*

Needed at Time of Preparation:

1½ lbs. ground beef

1 medium onion, chopped finely

1 cup dry bread crumbs *use gluten-free bread crumbs to make this recipe gluten-free

1 cup tomato juice

1 large egg or 2 small eggs

1 tsp. salt

scant ¼ tsp. black pepper

Preparation Instructions:

1. Place all ingredients into a gallon-sized freezer bag and smoosh until all ingredients are well-combined.

2. Remove as much air as possible and seal bag.

3. Label the bag with the information opposite, then freeze.

TIP: Leftover meatloaf makes great sandwiches! Or, freeze your leftover meatloaf slices into single portions for another day.

Guinness Corned Beef

*10 Ing. or Fewer *Quick to Prep

Bob Coffey, New Windsor, NY

Makes 10 servings

Prep. Time: 5 minutes ❧ Cooking Time: 8+ hours ❧ Ideal slow-cooker size: 5½-qt.

Needed at Time of Preparation:

3–4-lb. corned beef with seasoning packet

14.9-oz. can Guinness stout

¾ cup water

1 bay leaf

¼ tsp. mustard seeds

¼ tsp. caraway seeds

¼ tsp. peppercorns

Preparation Instructions:

1. Place all ingredients into a gallon-sized freezer bag.

2. Remove as much air as possible and seal bag.

3. Label the bag with the information below, then freeze.

TIP: If 10 servings is just too much for you, make it all and freeze the leftovers into portions appropriate for your family.

Information for Freezer Bag:

GUINNESS CORNED BEEF

Makes 10 servings

Cooking Time: 8+ hours ❧ Ideal slow-cooker size: 5½-qt.

Needed at Time of Cooking/ Serving:

1-lb. bag baby carrots

½ cup chopped onions

4 cups chopped cabbage

coarse mustard or horseradish, *optional*

Serving Suggestion: Serve with mashed potatoes.

Instructions:

1. Thaw bag completely for 24–48 hours or more.
2. Grease interior of slow-cooker crock.
3. Empty contents of freezer bag into crock.
4. Cover and cook on Low 8 hours, or until instant-read thermometer registers 145°F when stuck in center of meat.
5. One hour before end of cooking time, add carrots and onions.
6. Thirty minutes before end of cooking time, add chopped cabbage.
7. To serve, lift beef and vegetables out of liquid. (Save liquid for soup or cooking dried beans.) Discard bay leaf. Serve with coarse mustard or horseradish, with a side of mashed potatoes, if desired.

Pork Main Dishes

Garlic Pork Roast

*10 Ing. or Fewer *Gluten-Free–Optional

Earnie Zimmerman, Mechanicsburg, PA

Makes 10 servings

Prep. Time: 15–20 minutes ❧ Cooking Time: 6–8 hours ❧ Ideal slow-cooker size: 6- to 8-qt.

Needed at Time of Preparation:

3-lb. boneless pork loin roast, short and wide rather than long and narrow

1 tsp. salt

½ tsp. coarsely ground black pepper

1 medium onion, sliced

6 cloves garlic, peeled

8 strips (each 3 inches long, ½ inch wide) fresh lemon peel

1 lb. baby carrots

½ tsp. dried thyme

1 cup chicken broth *use a gluten-free brand to make this recipe gluten-free

Preparation Instructions:

1. Place all ingredients into a gallon-sized freezer bag and smoosh around to coat everything well.

2. Remove as much air as possible and seal bag.

3. Label the bag with the information below, then freeze.

TIP: If 10 servings is just too much for you, either split the recipe between 2–3 freezer bags or make it all and freeze the leftovers.

Information for Freezer Bag:

GARLIC PORK ROAST

Makes 10 servings

Cooking Time: 6–8 hours ❧ Ideal slow-cooker size: 6- to 8-qt.

Needed at Time of Cooking:

1½ lbs. red potatoes, cut in ½-inch-thick slices

Serving Suggestion: Serve with rice or couscous and a salad. *omit couscous if making this gluten-free

Instructions:

1. Thaw bag completely for 24–48 hours or more.
2. Grease interior of slow-cooker crock.
3. Place potatoes in bottom of crock, then empty the contents of the freezer bag on top.
4. Cover. Cook on Low 6–8 hours, or until instant-read meat thermometer registers 140–145°F when stuck in center of roast. Remove roast to cutting board. Cover to keep warm. Let stand for 10 minutes.
5. Check if onions, potatoes, and carrots are as tender as you like them. If not, cover crock and continue cooking another 30–60 minutes, or until veggies are as done as you want.
6. Slice pork into ½-inch-thick slices. Place on deep platter. Serve topped with vegetables and broth.

Cranberry Pork Roast

*10 Ing. or Fewer *Quick to Prep

Marcia S. Myer, Manheim, PA

Makes 4–6 servings

Prep. Time: 5 minutes ❦ Cooking Time: 6–8 hours ❦ Ideal slow-cooker size: 6-qt.

Needed at Time of Preparation:

2½–3-lb. boneless pork loin roast

16-oz. can whole berry cranberry sauce

¼ cup sugar

½ cup cranberry juice or water

1 tsp. dry mustard

¼ tsp. ground cloves

Preparation Instructions:

1. Place all ingredients into a gallon-sized freezer bag and smoosh around to coat the loin well.

2. Remove as much air as possible and seal bag.

3. Label the bag with the information below, then freeze.

Information for Freezer Bag:

CRANBERRY PORK ROAST

Makes 4–6 servings

Cooking Time: 6–8 hours ❦ Ideal slow-cooker size: 6-qt.

Needed at Time of Cooking:

2 Tbsp. cornstarch

2 Tbsp. cool water

Serving Suggestion: Mashed potatoes or noodles are good served with this recipe.

Instructions:

1. Thaw bag completely for 24–48 hours or more.

2. Empty contents of freezer bag into crock.

3. Cook on Low for 6–8 hours, or until the roast is tender. Transfer the roast to a plate and cover with foil to keep warm.

4. Skim the fat from the juices in the slow cooker. Measure 2 cups of the juice, adding water if needed to make 2 cups. Pour into a saucepan and bring to a boil over medium heat.

5. Mix the cornstarch in 2 Tbsp. cool water. When juice in the saucepan begins to boil, gradually add the cornstarch mixture and stir until thickened, about 4 minutes. Serve the cranberry gravy with the roast.

Savory Pork Roast

*10 Ing. or Fewer *Quick to Prep *Gluten-Free*

Mary Louise Martin, Boyd, WI

Makes 4–6 servings

Prep. Time: 5 minutes ❦ Cooking Time: 3½–4½ hours ❦ Ideal slow-cooker size: oval 6-qt.

Needed at Time of Preparation:

4-lb. boneless pork butt roast

1 tsp. ground ginger

1 Tbsp. fresh minced rosemary

½ tsp. mace

1 tsp. coarsely ground black pepper

2 tsp. salt

2 cups water

Preparation Instructions:

1. Place all ingredients into a gallon-sized freezer bag and smoosh around.

2. Remove as much air as possible and seal bag.

3. Label with the information below, then freeze.

Information for Freezer Bag:

SAVORY PORK ROAST

Makes 4–6 servings

Cooking Time: 3½–4½ hours ❦ Ideal slow-cooker size: oval 6-qt.

Instructions:

1. Thaw bag completely for 24–48 hours or more.

2. Grease interior of slow-cooker crock.

3. Empty contents of freezer bag into crock.

4. Cover. Cook on Low 3½–4½ hours, or until instant-read meat thermometer registers 140°F when stuck into center of roast.

HONEY-ORANGE PORK ROAST

Makes 8–10 servings

Cooking Time: 4–9½ hours

Needed at Time of Cooking:

4–5 good-sized sweet potatoes

2 good-sized tart apples

Instructions:

1. Thaw bag completely for 24–48 hours or more.

2. Grease interior of slow-cooker crock.

3. Empty contents of freezer bag into crock.

4. Cover. Cook on High 2–2½ hours, or on Low 4 hours.

5. While roast is cooking, peel sweet potatoes and cut into 1-inch-thick chunks. Place alongside and on top of roast.

6. Cover. Continue cooking 1 more hour on High, or 3 more hours on Low.

7. While roast and sweet potatoes are cooking, core and quarter apples.

8. Place apples alongside and on top of sweet potatoes.

9. Cover. Continue cooking another hour on High, or another 1–1½ hours on Low.

10. Insert instant-read meat thermometer into center of roast. When it reaches 150–160°F, roast is finished.

11. Check if sweet potatoes and apples are as tender as you like them. If not, remove roast to platter, cover, and keep warm. Continue cooking potatoes and apples another 30–60 minutes, or until done.

12. Slice roast against grain. Place slices of meat, sweet potatoes, and apples, along with broth, in deep platter or bowl to serve.

Honey-Orange Pork Roast

*5 Ing. or Fewer *Quick to Prep *Gluten-Free

Earnie Zimmerman, Mechanicsburg, PA

Makes 8–10 servings

Prep. Time: 5 minutes ❦ Cooking Time: 4—9½ hours ❦ Ideal slow-cooker size: oval 6- or 7-qt.

Needed at Time of Preparation:

4-lb. boneless pork butt roast

I cup orange juice

¼–½ cup honey

I cup fresh, frozen, or dried cranberries

Preparation Instructions:

1. Place all ingredients into a gallon-sized freezer bag and smoosh around to coat roast well.

2. Remove as much air as possible and seal bag.

3. Label the bag with the information opposite, then freeze.

TIP: If 8–10 servings is just too much for you, either split the recipe between 2 freezer bags or make it all and freeze the leftovers into portions appropriate for your family.

Roast Pork and Sauerkraut

Susan Alexander, Baltimore, MD

Makes 4–6 servings

Prep. Time: 15 minutes ❦ Cooking Time: 6–8 hours ❦ Ideal slow-cooker size: oval 6-qt.

Needed at Time of Preparation:

1–2 lbs. fresh or canned sauerkraut, depending on how much you like sauerkraut *make sure yours is gluten-free to make this recipe gluten-free

1 Tbsp. caraway seeds

1 large onion, sliced

3–4-lb. boneless pork butt roast

12-oz. can Coca-Cola

2 cups water

1 envelope dry onion soup mix *use a gluten-free brand to make this recipe gluten-free

Preparation Instructions:

1. Place all ingredients in a gallon-sized freezer bag.

2. Remove as much air as possible and seal bag.

3. Label the bag with the information below, then freeze.

Information for Freezer Bag:

ROAST PORK AND SAUERKRAUT

Makes 4–6 servings

Cooking Time: 6–8 hours ❦ Ideal slow-cooker size: oval 6-qt.

Serving Suggestion: This goes well with mashed potatoes, green beans, and cornbread.

Instructions:

1. Thaw bag completely for 24–48 hours or more.

2. Grease interior of slow-cooker crock.

3. Empty contents of freezer bag into crock.

4. Cover. Cook on Low 6–8 hours, or until instant-read meat thermometer registers 150°F when stuck in center of roast.

5. Cut meat into chunks and serve topped with sauerkraut, onion, seeds, and broth.

Brown-Sugar-and-Dijon Marinated Pork Roast

*5 Ing. or Fewer *Quick to Prep

J. B. Miller, Indianapolis, IN

Makes 4–6 servings

Prep. Time: 10 minutes ❧ Cooking Time: 3–3½ hours ❧ Ideal slow-cooker size: oval 5-qt.

Needed at Time of Preparation:

½ cup soy sauce

¼ cup sherry vinegar

½ tsp. Dijon mustard

¼ cup brown sugar

2-lb. pork loin roast, short and wide in shape

Preparation Instructions:

1. Place all ingredients into a gallon-sized freezer bag and smoosh around to coat loin well.

2. Remove as much air as possible and seal bag.

3. Label the bag with the information below, then freeze.

TIP: This recipes is so easy to assemble, you may want to consider doubling the ingredients now and making 2 freezer-bag meals instead of just 1.

Information for Freezer Bag:

BROWN-SUGAR-AND-DIJON MARINATED PORK ROAST

Makes 4–6 servings

Cooking Time: 3–3½ hours ❧ Ideal slow-cooker size: oval 5-qt.

Instructions:

1. Thaw bag completely for 24–48 hours or more.

2. Grease interior of slow-cooker crock.

3. Empty contents of freezer bag into crock.

4. Cover. Cook on Low for 3–3½ hours, or until an instant-read meat thermometer registers 140°F.

5. Slice and serve.

Teriyaki Pork Steak with Sugar Snap Peas

Hope Comerford, Clinton Township, MI

*10 Ing. or Fewer *Quick to Prep *Gluten-Free–Optional

Makes 4–6 servings

Prep. Time: 10 minutes ❧ Cooking Time: 7–9 hours ❧ Ideal slow-cooker size: 5-qt.

Needed at Time of Preparation:

2½-lb. pork shoulder blade steaks

1 Tbsp. onion powder

1 Tbsp. garlic powder

salt and pepper, to taste

1 cup teriyaki sauce *use a gluten-free brand to make this recipe gluten-free

½ medium onion, sliced into half rings

Preparation Instructions:

1. Place all ingredients into a gallon-sized freezer bag and smoosh around to coat pork well.

2. Remove as much air as possible and seal bag.

3. Label with the instructions below, then freeze.

TIP: This recipe is so easy to assemble, you may want to consider doubling the ingredients now and assembling 2 freezer-bag meals instead of just 1.

Information for Freezer Bag:

TERIYAKI PORK STEAK WITH SUGAR SNAP PEAS

Makes 4–6 servings

Cooking Time: 7–9 hours ❧ Ideal slow-cooker size: 5-qt.

Needed at Time of Cooking:

1½–2 cups sugar snap peas

Instructions:

1. Thaw bag completely for 24–48 hours or more.

2. Empty contents of freezer bag into crock.

3. Cover and cook on Low for 7–9 hours.

4. About 40 minutes before the cook time is up, add in the sugar snap peas.

5. Serve the pork with some of the sugar snap peas on top and sauce from the crock drizzled over the top.

Easy Pork Loin

*5 Ing. or Fewer *Quick to Prep *Gluten-Free–Optional

Colleen Heatwole, Burton, MI

Makes 4–5 servings

Prep. Time: 5 minutes ⚘ *Cooking Time: 3–5 hours* ⚘ *Ideal slow-cooker size: 3-qt.*

Needed at Time of Preparation:

1 ½-lb. pork loin

2 Tbsp. soy sauce *omit if making this gluten-free

2 Tbsp. tamari sauce *double this to 4 Tbsp. if making this recipe gluten-free

¼ tsp. ground ginger

½ tsp. garlic powder

Preparation Instructions:

1. In gallon-sized freezer bag place pork loin and all ingredients.

2. Seal bag and turn several times to cover meat with marinade.

3. Remove as much air as possible and seal bag again.

4. Label the bag with the information below, then freeze.

TIP: This recipe is so easy to assemble, you may want to consider doubling the ingredients now and assembling 2 freezer-bag meals instead of just 1.

Information for Freezer Bag:

EASY PORK LOIN

Makes 4–5 servings

Cooking Time: 3–5 hours ⚘ *Ideal slow-cooker size: 3-qt.*

Serving Suggestion: Goes well with sweet potatoes.

Instructions:

1. Thaw bag completely for 24–48 hours or more.

2. Empty contents of freezer bag into crock.

3. Cover and cook on Low 3–5 hours.

4. If desired, meat may be shredded to serve.

Savory Pork Loin

*10 Ing. or Fewer *Gluten-Free–Optional*

Colleen Heatwole, Burton, MI

Makes 6–8 servings

Prep. Time: 10 minutes ❧ Cooking Time: 6–8 hours ❧ Ideal slow-cooker size: 3- to 5-qt.

Needed at Time of Preparation:

3½-lb. pork loin

¼ cup soy sauce *replace with tamari or liquid aminos for gluten-free

¼ cup light brown sugar

½ cup tomato juice

1 Tbsp. lemon juice

1 tsp. Worcestershire sauce *make sure yours is gluten-free to make this recipe gluten-free

1½ cups water

Preparation Instructions:

1. Trim fat off pork loin.

2. Place all ingredients in gallon-sized freezer bag and smoosh around to make sure loin is coated well.

3. Remove as much air as possible and seal bag.

4. Label with the instructions below, then freeze.

TIP: If 6–8 servings is just too much for you, either split the recipe between 2 freezer bags or make it all and freeze the leftovers.

Information for Freezer Bag:

SAVORY PORK LOIN

Makes 6–8 servings

Cooking Time: 6–8 hours ❧ Ideal slow-cooker size: 3- to 5-qt.

Needed at Time of Serving:

hamburger buns

Instructions:

1. Thaw bag completely for 24–48 hours or more.

2. Empty contents of bag into crock.

3. Cover and cook on Low 6–8 hours.

4. If possible, turn several times to coat meat with sauce while cooking.

5. When done, shred meat and return to sauce.

6. Serve on hamburger buns.

TERRIFIC TENDERS

Makes 8 servings

Cooking Time: 3–4 hours ❦ *Ideal slow-cooker size: oval 6- or 7-qt.*

Needed at Time of Cooking/Serving:

1 Tbsp. butter

1 Tbsp. chopped shallots

1½ tsp. dried tarragon

1½ tsp. Dijon mustard *make sure yours is gluten-free to make this recipe gluten-free

fresh parsley sprigs

Instructions:

1. Thaw bag completely for 24–48 hours or more.

2. Grease interior of slow-cooker crock.

3. Remove meat from freezer bag, but reserve liquid in bag.

4. Cover cooker. Cook on Low 3–4 hours, or until instant-read meat thermometer registers 145°F when stuck in center of roast.

5. Near end of roast's cooking time, melt butter in skillet. Sauté shallots until softened. Stir in tarragon and mustard. Mix well.

6. Stir 1½–2 cups reserved marinade into mixture in skillet. Reduce heat and cook until slightly thickened and creamy. Set aside, but keep warm until serving time.

7. Remove roast from cooker to cutting board. Cover and keep warm. Let stand 10 minutes. Then slice.

8. Place slices in deep platter. Cover with warm sauce. Garnish with parsley sprigs and serve.

Terrific Tenders

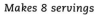

*5 Ing. or Fewer *Gluten-Free

Carol Turner, Mountain City, GA

Makes 8 servings

Prep. Time: 15–20 minutes ❧ Cooking Time: 3–4 hours ❧ Ideal slow-cooker size: oval 6- or 7-qt.

Needed at Time of Preparation:

3–4-lb. boneless pork loin roast, wide and short (not skinny and long)

7–9 cloves garlic, halved or quartered lengthwise

salt to taste

pepper to taste

2–2½ cups opal basil, raspberry or blackberry vinegar, or your favorite fruity vinegar

Preparation Instructions:

1. Pierce roast with knife about ½ inch deep at 2-inch intervals. Insert piece of garlic in each slit.

2. Place roast and all remaining ingredients into a gallon-sized freezer bag and smoosh around to coat roast well.

3. Remove as much air as possible and seal bag.

4. Label with the information opposite, then freeze.

TIP: If 8 servings is just too much for you, either split the recipe between 2 freezer bags or make it all and freeze the leftovers.

BARBECUED PULLED PORK

Makes 10–12 servings

Cooking Time: 4½–8½ hours ❦ *Ideal slow-cooker size: 5-qt.*

Needed at Time of Cooking/ Serving:

½ tsp. salt

1½ Tbsp. Worcestershire sauce *make sure yours is gluten-free if making this recipe gluten-free

¼ cup chopped onion

¼ cup brown sugar, packed

1 cup ketchup

¼ cup white vinegar

⅛ tsp. black pepper

1 Tbsp. prepared mustard

10–12 hamburger rolls *use gluten-free rolls to make this recipe gluten-free

Instructions:

1. Thaw bag completely for 24–48 hours or more.

2. Grease interior of slow-cooker crock.

3. Empty contents of freezer bag into crock.

4. Cover. Cook on Low 7½–8 hours, or on High 4–6 hours, or until instant-read meat thermometer stuck into center of roast registers 145–150°F.

5. Meanwhile, mix the salt, Worcestershire sauce, chopped onion, brown sugar, ketchup, white vinegar, black pepper, and prepared mustard together in a bowl. Set aside.

6. When roast is cooked, place it on a cutting board or in a roomy bowl. Using 2 forks, pull the pork apart, shredding it.

7. Return shredded pork to cooker. Stir in sauce and mix together well.

8. Cover. Cook on High 20–30 minutes, or until mixture reaches a boil.

9. Serve in hamburger rolls.

Barbecued Pulled Pork

*5 Ing. or Fewer *Quick to Prep *Gluten-Free–Optional

Sue Hertzler Schrag, Beatrice, NE

Makes 10–12 servings

Prep. Time: 30 minutes ❧ Cooking Time: 4½–8½ hours ❧ Ideal slow-cooker size: 5-qt.

Needed at Time of Preparation:

3–4-lb. boneless pork picnic shoulder roast

salt and pepper to taste

½ cup water

Preparation Instructions:

1. Place ingredients into a gallon-sized freezer bag.

2. Remove as much air as possible and seal bag.

3. Label with the information opposite, then freeze.

TIP: If 10–12 servings is just too much for you, either split the recipe between 2 freezer bags or make it all and freeze the leftovers into portions appropriate for your family.

PULLED PORK WITH DR PEPPER

Makes 6–8 sandwiches

Cooking Time: 4–8 hours ❦ *Ideal slow-cooker size: 6-qt.*

Needed at Time of Cooking:

your favorite barbecue sauce *make sure yours is gluten-free if you're making this recipe gluten-free

your favorite rolls or buns *use gluten-free buns or rolls if making this recipe gluten-free

Instructions:

1. Thaw bag completely for 24–48 hours or more.

2. Grease interior of slow-cooker crock.

3. Empty contents of freezer bag into crock.

4. Cover. Cook on Low 6–7 hours, or on High 3–4 hours, or until instant-read meat thermometer registers 145 –150°F when stuck into center of roast.

5. Using 2 sturdy metal spatulas, remove meat from crock and place on large cutting board. Using 2 forks, shred pork.

6. Place shredded pork back into crock. Mix well with sauce.

7. Cover. Cook 1 more hour on Low.

8. Using a slotted spoon, lift shredded meat and onion out of crock and into large bowl.

9. Stir barbecue sauce into meat and onion, ¼ cup at a time, until you get the sauciness you like.

10. Serve in rolls or buns.

Pulled Pork with Dr Pepper

*10 Ing. or Fewer *Gluten-Free–Optional*

Christina Gerber, Apple Creek, OH

Makes 6–8 sandwiches

Prep. Time: 20–25 minutes   ❧   Cooking Time: 4–8 hours   ❧   Ideal slow-cooker size: 6-qt.

Needed at Time of Preparation:

1 medium onion, cut in eighths

2½–3-lb. boneless pork butt roast

2 12-oz. cans Dr Pepper

1 clove garlic, minced

1½ tsp. dry mustard

¼–½ tsp. cayenne pepper, according to taste

1 tsp. salt

1 tsp. ground black pepper

¼ cup apple cider vinegar

3 Tbsp. Worcestershire sauce
*make sure yours is gluten-free to make this recipe gluten-free

Preparation Instructions:

1. Place all ingredients into a gallon-sized freezer bag and smoosh around to coat the roast well.

2. Remove as much air as possible, then seal bag.

3. Label the bag with the information opposite, then freeze.

TIP: If 6–8 servings is just too much for you, either split the recipe between 2 freezer bags or make it all and freeze the leftovers.

Korean-Inspired BBQ Shredded Pork

*Gluten-Free

Hope Comerford, Clinton Township, MI

Makes 8–10 servings
Prep. Time: 8–10 minutes ❦ Cooking Time: 8–10 hours ❦ Ideal slow-cooker size: 3-qt.

Needed at Time of Preparation:

1 medium onion

1 McIntosh apple, peeled, cored

5 cloves garlic

¼ cup rice vinegar

1 tsp. gluten-free hot sauce

2 Tbsp. low-sodium gluten-free soy sauce

1 Tbsp. ginger

1 Tbsp. chili powder

¼ tsp. red pepper flakes

3 Tbsp. brown sugar

1 cup ketchup

2–3-lb. pork sirloin tip roast

Preparation Instructions:

1. In a food processor, puree the onion, apple, and garlic. Pour this mixture in a bowl and mix it with the rice vinegar, hot sauce, soy sauce, ginger, chili powder, red pepper flakes, brown sugar, and ketchup.

2. Place the roast into a gallon-sized freezer bag and pour sauce you just pureed over the top. Smoosh around until roast is well coated.

3. Remove as much air as possible, then seal bag.

4. Label the bag with the information below, then freeze.

TIP: If 8–10 servings is just too much for you, either split the recipe between 2 freezer bags or make it all and freeze the leftovers into portions appropriate for your family.

Information for Freezer Bag:

KOREAN-INSPIRED BBQ SHREDDED PORK

Makes 8–10 servings
Cooking Time: 8–10 hours ❦ Ideal slow-cooker size: 3-qt.

Serving suggestion:

Serve over brown rice or quinoa with a side of bok choy sautéed in toasted sesame seed oil and red pepper flakes.

Instructions:

1. Thaw bag completely for 24–48 hours or more.

2. Empty contents of freezer bag into crock.

3. Cover and cook on Low 8–10 hours.

4. Remove the pork roast and shred it between 2 forks. Return the shredded pork to the crock and mix it through the sauce.

Spicy Pulled Pork Sandwiches

*5 Ing. or Fewer *Quick to Prep *Gluten-Free–Optional

Janie Steele, Moore, OK

Makes 8–10 servings

Prep. Time: 15–20 minutes ❧ Cooking Time: 8½–10½ hours ❧ Ideal slow-cooker size: 5-qt.

Needed at Time of Preparation:

4-lb. pork loin

14 oz. low-sodium beef broth *use gluten-free to make this recipe gluten-free

⅓ cup Worcestershire sauce *make sure yours is gluten-free to make this recipe gluten-free

⅓ cup hot sauce *make sure you choose a gluten-free hot sauce to make this recipe gluten-free

Preparation Instructions:

1. Place all ingredients into a gallon-sized freezer bag and smoosh around to coat loin well.

2. Remove as much air as possible and seal bag.

3. Label the bag with the information below, then freeze.

TIP: If 8–10 servings is just too much for you, either split the recipe between 2 freezer bags or make it all and freeze the leftovers into portions appropriate for your family.

Information for Freezer Bag:

SPICY PULLED PORK SANDWICHES

Makes 8–10 servings

Cooking Time: 8½–10½ hours ❧ Ideal slow-cooker size: 5-qt.

Needed at Time of Cooking/Serving:

½ cup Worcestershire sauce *make sure yours is gluten-free to make this recipe gluten-free

¼ cup hot sauce *make sure you choose a gluten-free hot sauce to make this recipe gluten-free

1 cup ketchup

1 cup molasses

½ cup mustard

kaiser rolls or buns of your choice *choose gluten-free buns or rolls to make this recipe gluten-free

Instructions:

1. Thaw bag completely for 24–48 hours or more.

2. Empty contents of freezer bag into crock.

3. Cover and cook 8–10 hours on Low. Remove meat, discard liquid.

4. Shred pork loin with two forks and return to slow cooker. Mix sauce and pour over meat and mix.

5. Cover and cook 30 minutes more or until heated through. Serve on buns.

Sweet Mustard Pulled Pork

*10 Ing. or Fewer *Quick to Prep *Gluten-Free–Optional

Jenny R. Unternahrer, Wayland, IA

Makes 6–10 servings

Prep. Time: 10 minutes ❦ Cooking Time: 8–9 hours ❦ Ideal slow-cooker size: 5- to 6-qt.

Needed at Time of Preparation:

1 cup yellow mustard

⅔ cup dark brown sugar

⅔ cup soy sauce (or soy-free substitute) *replace with tamari or liquid aminos to keep this recipe gluten-free

2 Tbsp. chili powder

½ tsp. dried onion powder

¼ cup apple cider vinegar

7-lb. pork shoulder (pork butt) roast, trimmed of fat and poked with a knife several times

Preparation Instructions:

1. Place all ingredients into a gallon-sized freezer bag and smoosh around to coat roast well.

2. Remove as much air as possible and seal bag.

3. Label bag with the information below, then freeze.

TIP: If 6–10 servings is just too much for you, either split the recipe between 2 freezer bags or make it all and freeze the leftovers into portions appropriate for your family.

Information for Freezer Bag:

SWEET MUSTARD PULLED PORK

Makes 6–10 servings

Cooking Time: 8–9 hours ❦ Ideal slow-cooker size: 5- to 6-qt.

Serving Suggestions: This is good served as is, or in a bun, tortilla, taco shell, or over buttered noodles with a side of cheesy veggies.

Instructions:

1. Thaw bag completely for 24–48 hours or more.

2. Empty contents of freezer bag into crock.

3. Cover and cook on Low for 8–9 hours, or until meat shreds easily with a fork. Remove pork from crock and shred.

4. Strain sauce through a sieve and pour over the meat. The meat will soak some of the sauce back up.

Salsa Verde Pork

*10 Ing. or Fewer *Gluten-Free–Optional

Hope Comerford, Clinton Township, MI

Makes 6 servings

Prep. Time: 20 minutes ❧ *Cooking Time: 6–6½ hours* ❧ *Ideal slow-cooker size: 4-qt.*

Needed at Time of Preparation:

1½ lb. boneless pork loin

1 large sweet onion, halved and sliced

2 large tomatoes, chopped

1 16-oz. jar salsa verde (green salsa)
*choose a gluten-free brand to keep
this recipe gluten-free

½ cup dry white wine

4 cloves garlic, minced

1 tsp. cumin

½ tsp. chili powder

Preparation Instructions:

1. Place all ingredients into a gallon-sized freezer bag and smoosh around to coat loin well.

2. Remove as much air as possible and seal bag.

3. Label the bag with the information below, then freeze.

Information for Freezer Bag:

SALSA VERDE PORK

Makes 6 servings

Cooking Time: 6–6½ hours ❧ *Ideal slow-cooker size: 4-qt.*

Serving Suggestion: Serve over cooked brown rice or quinoa.

Instructions:

1. Thaw bag completely for 24–48 hours or more.

2. Place contents of the freezer bag into the crock.

3. Cover and cook on Low for 6–6½ hours.

4. Break apart the pork with 2 forks and mix with contents of crock.

Carnitas

*10 Ing. or Fewer *Gluten-Free*

Hope Comerford, Clinton Township, MI

Makes 12 servings

Prep. Time: 10 minutes ❧ Cooking Time: 10–12 hours ❧ Ideal slow-cooker size: 4-qt.

Needed at Time of Preparation:

2-lb. pork shoulder roast

1 ½ tsp. kosher salt

½ tsp. pepper

2 tsp. cumin

5 cloves garlic, minced

1 tsp. oregano

3 bay leaves

2 cups gluten-free chicken stock

Preparation Instructions:

1. Place all ingredients into a gallon-sized freezer bag and smoosh around to coat roast well.

2. Remove as much air as possible and seal bag.

3. Label the bag with the information below, then freeze.

TIP: If 12 servings is just too much for you, either split the recipe between 3 freezer bags or make it all and freeze the leftovers into portions appropriate for your family.

Information for Freezer Bag:

CARNITAS

Makes 12 servings

Cooking Time: 10–12 hours ❧ Ideal slow-cooker size: 4-qt.

Needed at Time of Cooking/ Serving:

2 Tbsp. lime juice

1 tsp. lime zest

12 6-inch gluten-free white corn tortillas

Instructions:

1. Thaw bag completely for 24–48 hours or more.

2. Empty contents of freezer bag into crock.

3. Cover and cook on Low for 10–12 hours.

4. Remove the roast with a slotted spoon, as well as the bay leaves. Shred the pork between 2 forks, then replace the shredded pork in the crock and stir.

5. Add the lime juice and lime zest to the crock and stir.

6. Serve on warmed white corn tortillas.

Tasty Pork Tacos

*10 Ing. or Fewer *Gluten-Free

Donna Suter, Pandora, OH

Makes 6 servings

Prep. Time: 20 minutes ❧ Cooking Time: 6 hours ❧ Ideal slow-cooker size: 4-qt.

Needed at Time of Preparation:

3-lb. boneless pork butt roast

juice and zest of 2 limes

1–2 tsp. garlic powder,
or 1 tsp. minced garlic

½ tsp. salt

1–2 tsp. cumin

½ cup fresh chopped cilantro

Preparation Instructions:

1. Place all ingredients into a gallon-sized freezer bag and smoosh around until the roast is well-coated.

2. Remove as much air as possible and seal bag.

3. Label the bag with the information below, then freeze.

Information for Freezer Bag:

TASTY PORK TACOS

Makes 6 servings

Cooking Time: 6 hours ❧ Ideal slow-cooker size: 4-qt.

Needed at Time of Serving:

½ cup fresh chopped cilantro

gluten-free tortillas, hard or soft

salsa, *optional*

chopped onions, *optional*

chopped fresh tomatoes, *optional*

sliced black olives, *optional*

torn lettuce, *optional*

shredded cheese, *optional*

chopped jalapeño peppers, *optional*

sour cream, *optional*

Instructions:

1. Thaw bag completely for 24–48 hours or more.

2. Grease interior of slow-cooker crock.

3. Place contents of freezer bag into crock.

4. Cover. Cook on Low 6 hours, or until instant-read meat thermometer registers 145–150°F when inserted in center of roast.

5. Remove roast from crock and place in good-sized bowl. Shred, using 2 forks.

6. Stir shredded meat back into crock. Add chopped cilantro.

7. Fill tortillas and add your favorite toppings.

Pork Chops with Apples

*5 Ing. or Fewer *Gluten-Free

Arlene M. Kopp, Lineboro, MD

Makes 6 servings

Prep. Time: 15 minutes ❧ Cooking Time: 2–3 hours ❧ Ideal slow-cooker size: oval 6- or 7-qt.

Needed at Time of Preparation:

4 good-sized baking apples, cored and sliced, peeled or not

¼ cup brown sugar

1 tsp. cinnamon

6 ¾-inch-thick bone-in, blade-cut pork chops

salt to taste

pepper to taste

Preparation Instructions:

1. Place all ingredients into a gallon-sized freezer bag and smoosh around to coat everything well.

2. Remove as much air as possible and seal bag.

3. Label the bag with the information below, then freeze.

TIP: This recipe is so easy to assemble, you may want to consider doubling the ingredients now and assembling 2 freezer-bag meals instead of just 1.

Information for Freezer Bag:

PORK CHOPS WITH APPLES

Makes 6 servings

Cooking Time: 2–3 hours ❧ Ideal slow-cooker size: oval 6- or 7-qt.

Instructions:

1. Thaw bag completely 24–48 hours or more.

2. Grease interior of slow-cooker crock.

3. Empty contents of freezer bag into crock.

4. Cover. Cook on Low 2–3 hours, or until instant-read thermometer registers 140–145°F.

5. Serve on platter, topped with apples.

Chops in the Crock

Gluten-Free–Optional

Lavina Hochstedler, Grand Blanc, MI

Makes 4 servings

Prep. Time: 15–20 minutes 🍃 Cooking Time: 2½–3½ hours 🍃 Ideal slow-cooker size: 6- or 7-qt.

Needed at Time of Preparation:

4 ¾-inch-thick bone-in, blade-cut pork chops

salt and pepper to taste

2 medium onions, chopped

2 ribs celery, chopped

1 large green bell pepper, sliced

14½-oz. can stewed tomatoes, undrained

½ cup ketchup

2 Tbsp. cider vinegar

2 Tbsp. brown sugar

2 Tbsp. Worcestershire sauce *make sure yours is gluten-free to keep this recipe gluten-free

1 Tbsp. lemon juice

1 beef bouillon cube

Preparation Instructions:

1. Place all ingredients into a gallon-sized freezer bag and smoosh around to coat everything well.

2. Remove as much air as possible and seal bag.

3. Label the bag with the information below, then freeze.

Information for Freezer Bag:

CHOPS IN THE CROCK

Makes 4 servings

Cooking Time: 2½–3½ hours 🍃 Ideal slow-cooker size: 6- or 7-qt.

Needed at Time of Cooking/Serving:

2 Tbsp. cornstarch

2 Tbsp. water

cooked rice

Instructions:

1. Thaw bag completely for 24–48 hours or more.

2. Grease interior of slow-cooker crock.

3. Empty contents of freezer bag into crock and spread out.

4. Cover. Cook on Low 2–3 hours, or until instant-read meat thermometer registers 145°F when stuck into center of chops.

5. In small bowl, mix the cornstarch and water together until smooth. Stir into sauce in crock.

6. Cover. Cook 30 more minutes, until sauce thickens.

7. Serve over cooked rice.

Lemon Sweet Pork Chops

*10 Ing. or Fewer *Quick to Prep *Gluten-Free

Doris Slatten, Mount Juliet, TN

Makes 8 servings

Prep. Time: 5 minutes ❦ Cooking Time: 5–7 hours ❦ Ideal slow-cooker size: oval 7-qt.

Needed at Time of Preparation:

8 ¾-inch-thick bone-in, blade-cut pork chops

¼ tsp. salt

¼ tsp. coarsely ground black pepper

½ tsp. dried oregano

½ tsp. dried chives

⅓ tsp. dried dill

½ tsp. minced garlic

1 Tbsp. olive oil

Preparation Instructions:

1. Place all ingredients into a gallon-sized freezer bag and smoosh around until everything is well-coated.

2. Remove as much air as possible and seal bag.

3. Label the bag with the information below, then freeze.

TIP: If 8 servings is just too much for you, either split the recipe between 2 freezer bags or make it all and freeze the leftovers.

Information for Freezer Bag:

LEMON SWEET PORK CHOPS

Makes 8 servings

Cooking Time: 5–7 hours ❦ Ideal slow-cooker size: oval 7-qt.

Needed at Time of Cooking:

8 lemon slices

4 Tbsp. ketchup

4 Tbsp. brown sugar

Instructions:

1. Thaw bag completely for 24–48 hours or more.

2. Grease interior of slow-cooker crock.

3. Empty contents of freezer bag into crock and spread chops out.

4. Place lemon slice on each chop.

5. In same small bowl, mix together ketchup and brown sugar. Drop a Tbsp. of mixture on top of each chop.

6. Cover. Cook on Low 5–7 hours, or until instant-read meat thermometer registers 145°F when stuck into center of chops (but not against bone).

Raspberry Balsamic Pork Chops

*10 Ing. or Fewer *Quick to Prep *Gluten-Free

Hope Comerford, Clinton Township, MI

Makes 4–6 servings

Prep. Time: 5 minutes   ❦   Cooking Time: 7–8 hours   ❦   Ideal slow-cooker size: 3-qt.

Needed at Time of Preparations:

4–5 lbs. thick-cut pork chops

¼ cup raspberry balsamic vinegar

2 Tbsp. olive oil

½ tsp. kosher salt

½ tsp. garlic powder

¼ tsp. basil

¼ cup water

Preparation Instructions:

1. Place all ingredients into a gallon-sized freezer bag and smoosh around.

2. Remove as much air as possible and seal bag.

3. Label with the information below, then freeze.

TIP: This recipe is so easy to assemble, you may want to consider doubling the ingredients now and preparing 2 freezer-bag meals instead of just 1.

Information for Freezer Bag:

RASPBERRY BALSAMIC PORK CHOPS

Makes 4–6 servings

Cooking Time: 7–8 hours   ❦   Ideal slow-cooker size: 3-qt.

Serving Suggestion: Goes well with a salad and baked sweet potatoes.

Instructions:

1. Thaw bag completely for 24–48 hours or more.

2. Empty contents of freezer bag into crock and spread chops out.

3. Cover and cook on Low for 7–8 hours.

Brown Sugar Pork Chops

*10 Ing. or Fewer *Gluten-Free–Optional

Andrea Maher, Dunedin, FL

Makes 6 servings

Prep. Time: 5 minutes ❦ Cooking Time: 3–8 hours ❦ Ideal slow-cooker size: 5- or 6-qt.

Needed at Time of Preparation:

2 Tbsp. garlic powder

2 tsp. Dijon mustard *make sure yours is gluten-free to keep this recipe gluten-free

3 Tbsp. apple cider vinegar

¼ teaspoon pepper

¼ teaspoon kosher salt

⅓ cup water

¼ cup brown sugar or ¼ cup sugar-free maple syrup

3 cups pineapple slices

24 oz. pork chops

½ cup chopped celery

Preparation Instructions:

1. Place all ingredients into a gallon-sized freezer bag and smoosh around to coat everything well.

2. Remove as much air as possible and seal bag.

3. Label with the information below, then freeze.

Information for Freezer Bag:

BROWN SUGAR PORK CHOPS

Makes 6 servings

Cooking Time: 3–8 hours ❦ Ideal slow-cooker size: 5- or 6-qt.

Instructions:

1. Thaw bag completely for 24–48 hours or more.

2. Empty contents of freezer bag into crock and spread chops out.

3. Cover and cook on High for 3–4 hours or on Low for 6–8 hours.

Pork Chops with Asian Flair

*10 Ing. or Fewer

Shirley Unternahrer, Wayland, IA

Makes 4 servings

Prep. Time: 15 minutes 🌱 Cooking Time: 2–3 hours 🌱 Ideal slow-cooker size: 4- to 6-qt.

Needed at Time of Preparation:

½ cup orange juice

½ cup orange marmalade

2 cloves garlic, minced

3 Tbsp. soy sauce

2 Tbsp. brown sugar

2 Tbsp. rice vinegar,
or 1 Tbsp. white vinegar

2 tsp. Asian-style chili paste

4 6–7-oz. bone-in,
blade-cut pork chops

Preparation Instructions:

1. Place all ingredients into a gallon-sized freezer bag and smoosh around to coat chops well.

2. Remove as much air as possible and seal bag.

3. Label the bag with the information below, then freeze.

Information for Freezer Bag:

PORK CHOPS WITH ASIAN FLAIR

Makes 4 servings

Cooking Time: 2–3 hours 🌱 Ideal slow-cooker size: 4- to 6-qt.

Needed at Time of Cooking/Serving:

8 oz. angel-hair pasta

8 oz. snow peas or broccoli

Instructions:

1. Thaw bag completely for 24–48 hours or more.

2. Grease interior of slow-cooker crock.

3. Empty contents of freezer bag into crock and spread chops out.

4. Cover. Cook 2–3 hours on Low, or until instant-read meat thermometer registers 145–150°F when stuck in center of chops (but not against bone).

5. Near end of cooking time for chops, cook pasta according to package directions.

6. Two minutes before end of pasta cooking time, stir snow peas or broccoli into water with pasta. When done cooking, drain and keep warm.

7. Place chops on platter.

8. Toss pasta and snow peas with sauce in crock. Spoon onto serving platter next to chops. Serve.

Boneless Barbecued Pork Ribs

*5 Ing. or Fewer *Quick to Prep *Gluten-Free–Optional

Jessalyn Wantland, Paris, TX

Makes 4–6 servings

Prep. Time: 10 minutes ❧ Cooking Time: 5–6 hours ❧ Ideal slow-cooker size: 5- or 6-qt.

Needed at Time of Preparation:

3–4 lbs. boneless pork ribs

1 onion, sliced

2 cups your favorite barbecue sauce
*make sure yours is gluten-free to keep
this recipe gluten-free

2 tsp. lemon juice

Preparation Instructions:

1. Place all ingredients into a gallon-sized freezer bag and smoosh around to coat ribs well.

2. Remove as much air as possible and seal bag.

3. Label bag with the information below, then freeze.

TIP: This recipe is so easy to assemble, you may want to consider doubling the ingredients now and preparing 2 freezer-bag meals instead of just 1.

Information for Freezer Bag:

BONELESS BARBECUED PORK RIBS

Makes 4–6 servings

Cooking Time: 5–6 hours ❧ Ideal slow-cooker size: 5- or 6-qt.

Serving Suggestion: Goes well with corn on the cob.

Instructions:

1. Thaw bag completely for 24–48 hours or more.

2. Grease interior of slow-cooker crock.

3. Empty contents of freezer bag into crock and spread out ribs.

4. Cover and cook on Low 5–6 hours, or until instant-read meat thermometer registers 150°F when stuck in center of ribs.

Saucy Spareribs

Gluten-Free–Optional

Phyllis Good, Lancaster, PA

Makes 4 servings

Prep. Time: 15 minutes ❧ Cooking Time: 4–5 hours ❧ Ideal slow-cooker size: 6-qt.

Needed at Time of Preparation:

3–4 lbs. country-style pork spareribs, cut into serving-sized pieces

¾ cup ketchup

1-2 Tbsp. sriracha sauce, depending how much heat you like, *optional* *make sure yours is gluten-free to keep this recipe gluten-free

3 Tbsp. packed brown sugar

¼ cup honey

¼ cup lemon juice

2 Tbsp. soy sauce *use gluten-free soy sauce or tamari to keep this gluten-free

¾ tsp. ground ginger

¼ tsp. chili powder

¼ tsp. ground mustard

¼ tsp. garlic powder

¼ tsp. black pepper (coarsely ground is best)

Preparation Instructions:

1. Place all ingredients into a gallon-sized freezer bag and smoosh around until everything is well-coated.

2. Remove as much air as possible and seal bag.

3. Label the bag with the information below, then freeze.

Information for Freezer Bag:

SAUCY SPARERIBS

Makes 4 servings

Cooking Time: 4–5 hours ❧ Ideal slow-cooker size: 6-qt.

Instructions:

1. Thaw bag completely for 24–48 hours or more.

2. Empty contents of freezer bag into crock and spread ribs out.

3. Cover and cook on Low 4–6 hours, or until the meat begins to fall off the bones.

Sweet-and-Sour Ribs

*Gluten-Free–Optional

Frances Kruba, Baltimore, MD

Makes 8 servings

Prep. Time: 20 minutes ❦ Cooking Time: 5–8 hours ❦ Ideal slow-cooker size: oval 6-qt.

Needed at Time of Preparation:

3–4 lbs. spareribs, cut to fit into a gallon-sized freezer bag

20-oz. can pineapple tidbits, undrained

2 8-oz. cans tomato sauce

½ cup thinly sliced onions

½ cup thinly sliced green bell pepper

½ cup packed brown sugar

¼ cup cider vinegar

¼ cup tomato paste or ketchup

2 Tbsp. Worcestershire sauce
*make sure yours is gluten-free to keep this recipe gluten-free

1 clove garlic, minced

salt and pepper to taste

Preparation Instructions:

1. Place all ingredients into a gallon-sized freezer bag and smoosh around until ribs are well-coated.

2. Remove as much air as possible and seal bag.

3. Label the bag with the information below, then freeze.

TIP: If 8 servings is just too much for you, either split the recipe between 2 freezer bags or make it all and freeze the leftovers.

Information for Freezer Bag:

SWEET-AND-SOUR RIBS

Makes 8 servings

Cooking Time: 5–8 hours ❦ Ideal slow-cooker size: oval 6-qt.

Instructions:

1. Thaw bag completely for 24–48 hours or more.
2. Empty contents of bag in crock, spreading the ribs out.
3. Cover. Cook on Low 5–8 hours or until meat is tender.
4. Remove ribs from sauce and keep warm.
5. Using a good-sized spoon, lift layer of grease off sauce and discard. Or refrigerate sauce, allowing fat to harden. Then remove with spoon.
6. After removing grease, heat sauce and serve with ribs.

Easiest-Ever Country Ribs

*5 Ing. or Fewer *Quick to Prep *Gluten-Free–Optional

Hope Comerford, Clinton Township, MI

Makes 4–6 servings

Prep. Time: 5 minutes ❦ Cooking Time: 8–10 hours ❦ Ideal slow-cooker size: 6-qt.

Needed at Time of Preparation:

4 lbs. boneless country ribs

salt and pepper, to taste

18-oz. bottle of your favorite barbecue sauce *make sure yours is gluten-free to keep this recipe gluten-free

Preparation Instructions:

1. Place all ingredients into a gallon-sized freezer bag and smoosh around to coat all ribs evenly.

2. Remove as much air as possible and seal bag.

3. Label the bag with the information below, then freeze.

TIP: This recipe is so easy to assemble, you may want to consider doubling the ingredients now and assembling 2 freezer-bag meals instead of just 1.

Information for Freezer Bag:

EASIEST-EVER COUNTRY RIBS

Makes 4–6 servings

Cooking Time: 8–10 hours ❦ Ideal slow-cooker size: 6-qt.

Instructions:

1. Thaw bag completely for 24–48 hours or more.

2. Empty contents of freezer bag into crock and spread ribs out evenly.

3. Cover and cook on Low for 8–10 hours.

Country-Style Ribs

*10 Ing. or Fewer *Gluten-Free–Optional

Patricia Howard, Green Valley, AZ

Makes 6–8 servings

Prep. Time: 10–15 minutes ❧ Cooking Time: 3–7 hours ❧ Ideal slow-cooker size: 6-qt.

Needed at Time of Preparation:

4–5 lbs. pork shoulder ribs, cut into pieces that will fit in a gallon-sized freezer bag

¾ cup ketchup

¾ cup water

1 tsp. salt

1 tsp. coarsely ground black pepper

dash cayenne pepper

1 Tbsp. chopped dried chile

2 Tbsp. apple cider vinegar

2 Tbsp. Worcestershire sauce
*make sure yours is gluten-free to keep this recipe gluten-free

Preparation Instructions:

1. Place all ingredients into a gallon-sized freezer bag and smoosh around to coat all ribs evenly.

2. Remove as much air as possible and seal bag.

3. Label the bag with the information below, then freeze.

TIP: If 6–8 servings is just too much for you, either split the recipe between 2 freezer bags or make it all and freeze the leftovers.

Information for Freezer Bag:

COUNTRY-STYLE RIBS

Makes 6–8 servings

Cooking Time: 3–7 hours ❧ Ideal slow-cooker size: 6-qt.

Instructions:

1. Thaw bag completely for 24–48 hours or more.

2. Empty contents of freezer bag into crock. If you need to make a second layer, stagger pieces so they don't directly overlap each other.

3. Cover. Cook on Low 5–7 hours, or on High 3–4 hours, or until instant-read meat thermometer registers 145–150°F when stuck in center of ribs (but not against bone).

Barbecued Ham Steaks

*10 Ing. or Fewer *Gluten-Free

Phyllis Good, Lancaster, PA

Makes 4 servings

Prep. Time: 15 minutes ❦ Cooking Time: 3–4 hours ❦ Ideal slow-cooker size: oval 6- or 7-qt.

Needed at Time of Preparation:

1 small onion, chopped

7-oz. bottle 7-Up, Sprite, or ginger ale

¼ cup ketchup

1 tsp. dry mustard

1 tsp. salt

⅓ tsp. black pepper

4 whole cloves

2 lbs. ham steaks

Preparation Instructions:

1. Place all ingredients into a gallon-sized freezer bag and smoosh around.

2. Remove as much air as possible and seal bag.

3. Label the bag with the information below, then freeze.

Information for Freezer Bag:

BARBECUED HAM STEAKS

Makes 4 servings

Cooking Time: 3–4 hours ❦ Ideal slow-cooker size: oval 6 or 7-qt.

Instructions:

1. Thaw bag completely for 24–48 hours or more.

2. Empty contents of freezer bag in crock. Overlap steaks if you must, but as little as possible.

3. Cover and cook on Low 3–4 hours, or until meat is heated through but not dry.

4. Fish out cloves and discard.

5. Cut each steak into smaller pieces and serve topped with barbecue sauce.

Polish Kraut and Apples

*10 Ing. or Fewer *Gluten-Free–Optional

Frances Kruba, Baltimore, MD

Makes 4 servings

Prep. Time: 10–15 minutes 🌿 Cooking Time: 2–5 hours 🌿 Ideal slow-cooker size: 5-qt.

Needed at Time of Preparation:

14½-oz. can sauerkraut, drained, divided *make sure yours is gluten-free to make this recipe gluten-free

1 lb. fully cooked Polish sausage, cut in 1-inch-thick pieces *make sure yours is gluten-free to make this recipe gluten-free

3 medium tart apples, peeled and cut into eighths

½ cup packed brown sugar

½ tsp. caraway seeds

⅛ tsp. coarsely ground black pepper

¾ cup apple juice

Preparation Instructions:

1. Place all ingredients into a gallon-sized freezer bag and smoosh around.

2. Remove as much air as possible and seal bag.

3. Label the bag with the information below, then freeze.

Information for Freezer Bag:

POLISH KRAUT AND APPLES

Makes 4 servings

Cooking Time: 2–5 hours 🌿 Ideal slow-cooker size: 5-qt.

Instructions:

1. Thaw bag completely for 24–48 hours or more.

2. Grease interior of slow-cooker crock.

3. Empty contents of freezer bag into crock.

4. Cover. Cook on Low 4–5 hours or on High 2–2½ hours, or until apples are tender and everything is heated through.

Polish Sausage and Sauerkraut

*10 Ing. or Fewer *Gluten-Free–Optional*

Hope Comerford, Clinton Township, MI

Makes 4–6 servings

Prep. Time: 25 minutes 🌱 Cooking Time: 6–7 hours 🌱 Ideal slow-cooker size: 6-qt.

Needed at Time of Preparation:

27 oz. Polish sausage, cut into 1½-inch angled pieces *make sure yours is gluten-free to make this recipe gluten-free

4 slices of cooked bacon, chopped *make sure yours is gluten-free to make this recipe gluten-free

2 Golden Delicious apples, peeled and cut into thin slices

2 lbs. sauerkraut, drained and rinsed well *make sure yours is gluten-free to make this recipe gluten-free

½ large red onion, sliced

1 bay leaf

2 cloves garlic, minced

2 Tbsp. brown sugar

12 oz. dark beer *use a gluten-free beer to make this recipe gluten-free

Preparation Instructions:

1. Place all ingredients into a gallon-sized freezer bag and smoosh around.

2. Remove as much air as possible and seal bag.

3. Label the bag with the information below, then freeze.

Information for Freezer Bag:

POLISH SAUSAGE AND SAUERKRAUT

Makes 4–6 servings

Cooking Time: 6–7 hours 🌱 Ideal slow-cooker size: 6-qt.

Instructions:

1. Thaw bag completely for 24–48 hours or more.

2. Empty contents of freezer bag into crock.

3. Cover and cook on Low for 6–7 hours.

4. When you are ready to serve, remove the bay leaf and discard it.

Sweet-and-Sour Kielbasa

*5 Ing. or Fewer *Quick to Prep *Gluten-Free–Optional

Phyllis Good, Lancaster, PA

Makes 8–10 servings

Prep. Time: 5 minutes 🌿 Cooking Time: 4 hours 🌿 Ideal slow-cooker size: 5- or 6-qt.

Needed at Time of Preparation:

3 lbs. kielbasa,
cut into 1-inch-thick slices

1 bottle chili sauce *choose
a gluten-free brand to keep
this recipe gluten-free

20-oz. can crushed
pineapple, undrained

½ cup brown sugar

Preparation Instructions:

1. Place all ingredients into a gallon-sized freezer bag and smoosh around to coat all well.

2. Remove as much air as possible and seal bag.

3. Label the bag with the information below, then freeze.

TIP: If 8–10 servings is just too much for you, either split the recipe between 2–3 freezer bags or make it all and freeze the leftovers into portions appropriate for your family.

Information for Freezer Bag:

SWEET-AND-SOUR KIELBASA

Makes 8–10 servings

Cooking Time: 4 hours 🌿 Ideal slow-cooker size: 5- or 6-qt.

Needed at Time of Serving:

cooked rice, pasta, or potatoes

Instructions:

1. Thaw bag completely for 24–48 hours or more.

2. Empty contents of freezer bag into crock.

3. Cover. Cook on Low 4 hours, or until kielbasa is fully cooked.

4. Serve over cooked rice, pasta, or potatoes.

Hearty Sausage and Beans

*10 Ing. or Fewer *Gluten-Free–Optional

Sharon Shank, Bridgewater, VA

Makes 12 servings

Prep. Time: 10 minutes ❧ *Cooking Time: 2–4 hours* ❧ *Ideal slow-cooker size: 6-qt.*

Needed at Time of Preparation:

2 quarts sauerkraut, drained, with ½ cup juice reserved *make sure yours is gluten-free to make this recipe gluten-free

1 lb. smoked sausage, cut into small pieces *choose a gluten-free brand to make this recipe gluten-free

½ medium onion, chopped

3 15½-oz. cans pinto or navy beans

¼ cup brown sugar

½ cup ketchup

¼–½ tsp. coarsely ground pepper

Preparation Instructions:

1. Place all ingredients into a gallon-sized freezer bag and gently smoosh around.

2. Remove as much air as possible and seal bag.

3. Label the bag with the information below, then freeze.

TIP: If 12 servings is just too much for you, either split the recipe between 2 freezer bags or make it all and freeze the leftovers into portions appropriate for your family.

Information for Freezer Bag:

HEARTY SAUSAGE AND BEANS

Makes 12 servings

Cooking Time: 2–4 hours ❧ *Ideal slow-cooker size: 6-qt.*

Instructions:

1. Thaw bag completely for 24–48 hours or more.

2. Empty contents of freezer bag into crock.

3. Cover. Cook on Low for 4 hours or on High 2 hours.

Jiffy Jambalaya

Gluten-Free–Optional

Carole M. Mackie, Williamsfield, IL

Makes 6 servings

Prep. Time: 30 minutes ❧ Cooking Time: 4–5 hours ❧ Ideal slow-cooker size: 5-qt.

Needed at Time of Preparation:

1 onion, chopped

½ cup chopped green bell pepper

1 lb. smoked sausage, sliced into 1-inch-thick slices *make sure yours is gluten-free to keep this recipe gluten-free

28-oz. can diced tomatoes, undrained

½ cup water

1 Tbsp. sugar

1 tsp. paprika

½ tsp. dried thyme

½ tsp. dried oregano

¼ tsp. garlic powder

3 drops hot pepper sauce
*make sure yours is gluten-free
to keep this recipe gluten-free

Preparation Instructions:

1. Place all ingredients into a gallon-sized freezer bag and smoosh around to coat everything well.

2. Remove as much air as possible and seal bag.

3. Label the bag with the information below, then freeze.

Information for Freezer Bag:

JIFFY JAMBALAYA

Makes 6 servings

Cooking Time: 4–5 hours ❧ Ideal slow-cooker size: 5-qt.

Needed at Time of Cooking:

1½ cups uncooked instant rice

Instructions:

1. Thaw bag completely for 24–48 hours or more.

2. Grease interior of slow-cooker crock.

3. Empty contents of freezer bag into crock.

4. Cover. Cook on Low 3 hours, or until vegetables are as tender as you like them.

5. Stir in rice. Cover. Cook on High 20–30 minutes, or until rice is tender and fully cooked.

6. Stir and serve.

Meatless & Seafood Main Dishes

MEATLESS MAIN DISHES

Jamaican Rice and Beans

*10 Ing. or Fewer *Quick to Prep *Gluten-Free *Vegetarian *Vegan

Lorraine Pflederer, Goshen, IN

Makes 4 servings

Prep. Time: 10 minutes ❧ Cooking Time: 2 hours ❧ Ideal slow-cooker size: 3-qt.

Needed at Time of Preparation:

½ cup water

scant ½ tsp. allspice

½ tsp. salt

3 fresh thyme sprigs,
or 1 tsp. dried thyme

1 clove garlic, crushed

15-oz. can dark red kidney beans,
drained and rinsed

Preparation Instructions:

1. Place all ingredients into a gallon-sized freezer bag.

2. Remove as much air as possible, then seal bag.

3. Label the bag with the information below, then freeze.

TIP: This recipe is so easy to assemble, you may want to consider doubling the ingredients now and preparing 2 freezer-bag meals instead of just 1.

Information for Freezer Bag:

JAMAICAN RICE AND BEANS

Makes 4 servings

Cooking Time: 2 hours ❧ Ideal slow-cooker size: 3-qt.

Needed at Time of Cooking:

14-oz. can light coconut milk

1 cup uncooked instant rice

Instructions:

1. Thaw bag completely for 24–48 hours or more.

2. Grease interior of slow-cooker crock.

3. Empty contents of freezer bag into crock and stir in the coconut milk.

4. Cover. Cook on Low 1½ hours.

5. Stir rice into crock.

6. Cover. Cook on High 20–30 minutes, or until rice is tender but not dry.

7. Stir and serve.

Mexican Rice and Beans

*10 Ing. or Fewer *Quick to Prep *Gluten-Free–Optional *Vegetarian *Vegan

Helen Schlabach, Winesburg, OH

Makes 6–8 servings

Prep. Time: 10 minutes ❧ Cooking Time: 2–3 hours ❧ Ideal slow-cooker size: 4-qt.

Needed at Time of Preparation:

15-oz. can black beans, rinsed and drained

10-oz. pkg. frozen whole-kernel corn

16-oz. jar thick and chunky mild or medium salsa *make sure yours is gluten-free to keep this recipe gluten-free

1½ cups vegetable, tomato cocktail, or tomato juice

½ tsp. dried cumin

½ tsp. dried oregano

½ tsp. salt

¼ tsp. black pepper

Preparation Instructions:

1. Place all ingredients into a gallon-sized freezer bag.

2. Remove as much air as possible and seal bag.

3. Label the bag with the information below, then freeze.

TIP: If 6–8 servings is just too much for you, either split the recipe between 2 freezer bags or make it all and freeze the leftovers.

Information for Freezer Bag:

MEXICAN RICE AND BEANS

Makes 6–8 servings

Cooking Time: 2–3 hours ❧ Ideal slow-cooker size: 4-qt.

Needed at Time of Cooking:

1 cup raw long-grain brown rice

¾ cup shredded cheddar cheese *sub for vegan

Instructions:

1. Thaw bag completely for 24–48 hours or more.

2. Grease interior of slow-cooker crock.

3. Empty contents of freezer bag into crock and stir in long-grain brown rice.

4. Cover. Cook on High 2–3 hours, until rice is tender, stirring once halfway through.

5. Scatter cheese over rice and beans.

6. Allow to stand, uncovered, until cheese melts.

Quinoa and Black Beans

*10 Ing. or Fewer *Gluten-Free *Vegetarian *Vegan*

Gloria Frey, Lebanon, PA

Makes 6–8 servings

Prep. Time: 15–20 minutes ❧ *Cooking Time: 2–3 hours* ❧ *Ideal slow-cooker size: 4-qt.*

Needed at Time of Preparation:

1 medium onion, chopped

3 cloves garlic, chopped

1 red bell pepper, chopped

1½ cups vegetable broth
*make sure yours is gluten-free
to keep this recipe gluten-free

1 tsp. ground cumin

¼ tsp. cayenne pepper

½ tsp. salt

¼ tsp. coarsely ground black pepper

1 cup fresh, frozen, or drained canned corn

2 15-oz. cans black beans,
rinsed and drained

Preparation Instructions:

1. Add all ingredients into a gallon-sized freezer bag.

2. Remove as much air as possible and seal bag.

3. Label the bag with the information below, then freeze.

TIP: If 6–8 servings is just too much for you, either split the recipe between 2 freezer bags or make it all and freeze the leftovers.

Information for Freezer Bag:

QUINOA AND BLACK BEANS

Makes 6–8 servings

Cooking Time: 2–3 hours ❧ *Ideal slow-cooker size: 4-qt.*

Needed at time of Cooking/Serving:

¾ cup uncooked quinoa

½ cup fresh cilantro, chopped

Instructions:

1. Thaw bag completely for 24–48 hours or more.

2. Grease interior of slow-cooker crock.

3. Empty contents of bag into crock.

4. Cover. Cook on Low 2 hours, or until veggies are as tender as you like.

5. Stir in quinoa. Cover and continue cooking on Low 20–30 more minutes, or until quinoa is tender.

6. Just before serving, stir in cilantro.

Vegetarian Coconut Curry

*10 Ing. or Fewer *Gluten-Free *Vegetarian *Vegan

Hope Comerford, Clinton Township, MI

Makes 10–14 servings

Prep. Time: 30 minutes ❦ Cooking Time: 4–5 hours ❦ Ideal slow-cooker size: 7-qt.

Needed at Time of Preparation:

2 cups chopped broccoli

2 cups peeled and cubed butternut squash

I cup chopped carrots

¾ cup chopped onion

¾ cup chopped celery

½ cup chopped mushrooms

15½-oz. can garbanzo beans, drained and rinsed

24-oz. container of coconut curry sauce (or any other type of curry sauce you enjoy)

Preparation Instructions:

1. Place all ingredients into a gallon-sized freezer bag.

2. Remove as much air as possible and seal bag.

3. Label the bag with the information below, then freeze.

TIP: If 10–14 servings is just too much for you, either split the recipe between 2 freezer bags or make it all and freeze the leftovers into portions appropriate for your family.

Information for Freezer Bag:

VEGETARIAN COCONUT CURRY

Makes 10–14 servings

Cooking Time: 4–5 hours ❦ Ideal slow-cooker size: 7-qt.

Needed at Time of Serving:

cooked rice or pasta *use gluten-free pasta to keep this recipe gluten-free

Instructions:

1. Thaw bag completely for 24–48 hours or more.

2. Empty contents of bag into crock.

3. Cover and cook on Low for 4–5 hours, or until vegetables are as tender as you like them.

4. Serve over cooked rice or pasta.

Salsa Lentils

*10 Ing. or Fewer *Gluten-Free–Optional *Vegetarian *Vegan*

Karen Stanley, Amherst, VA

Makes 4 servings

Prep. Time: 15 minutes ❧ Cooking Time: 2–4 hours ❧ Ideal slow-cooker size: 4- or 5-qt.

Needed at Time of Preparation:

2 cups dry green lentils,
picked over for any stones and rinsed

4 cups water

2 cups chopped onions

¼ cup chopped garlic

2 cups salsa, mild, medium,
or hot *make sure yours is gluten-free
to keep this recipe gluten-free

1–3 jalapeño peppers,
seeded and chopped

1¼-oz. pkg. dry taco seasoning *make
sure yours is gluten-free to keep this
recipe gluten-free

½ tsp. salt

Preparation Instructions:

1. Place all ingredients into a gallon-sized freezer bag.

2. Remove as much air as possible and seal bag.

3. Label the bag with the information below, then freeze.

Information for Freezer Bag:

SALSA LENTILS

Makes 4 servings

Cooking Time: 2–4 hours ❧ Ideal slow-cooker size: 4- or 5-qt.

Needed at Time of Cooking/Serving:

1 cup chopped fresh cilantro

cooked rice or corn chips

chopped lettuce, *optional*

diced fresh tomatoes, *optional*

grated cheese of your choice, *optional*

sour cream, *optional, omit for a vegan recipe*

Instructions:

1. Thaw bag completely for 24–48 hours or more.

2. Grease interior of slow-cooker crock.

3. Empty contents of freezer bag into crock.

4. Cover. Cook on Low 3–4 hours or on High 2–3 hours, or until lentils are tender.

5. Just before serving, stir in chopped cilantro.

6. Serve over rice or corn chips.

7. Top with remaining optional ingredients.

Lentils Swiss-Style

*Vegetarian

Lenore Waltner, North Newton, KS

Makes 6 servings

Prep. Time: 20–30 minutes   ❧   Cooking Time: 2–6 hours   ❧   Ideal slow-cooker size: 5-qt.

Needed at Time of Preparation:

1 ¾ cups dry lentils,
picked over for any stones and rinsed

2 cups water

1 whole bay leaf

2 tsp. salt

¼ tsp. coarsely ground black pepper

½ tsp. dried marjoram

½ tsp. dried sage

½ tsp. dried thyme

2 large onions, chopped

2–4 cloves garlic, minced

2 cups home-canned tomatoes, or 1 14½-oz. can diced or stewed tomatoes

2 large carrots, sliced thinly

½ cup celery, sliced thinly

Preparation Instructions:

1. Place all ingredients into a gallon-sized freezer bag.

2. Remove as much air as possible and seal bag.

3. Label the bag with the information below, then freeze.

Information for Freezer Bag:

LENTILS SWISS-STYLE

Makes 6 servings

Cooking Time: 2–6 hours   ❧   Ideal slow-cooker size: 5-qt.

Needed at Time of Cooking/ Serving:

1 green bell pepper, chopped, *optional*

¼ cup chopped fresh parsley

¼ cup sherry

3 cups shredded Swiss or cheddar cheese

Instructions:

1. Thaw bag completely for 24–48 hours or more.

2. Grease interior of slow-cooker crock.

3. Empty contents of bag into crock and stir.

4. Cover. Cook on Low 4–6 hours, or on High 2–3 hours, or until lentils and raw vegetables are as tender as you like them.

5. Twenty minutes before end of cooking time, stir in chopped green pepper, if using.

6. Just before serving, stir in parsley and sherry. Sprinkle with cheese.

Lentil Tacos

*10 Ing. or Fewer *Gluten-Free *Vegetarian–Optional *Vegan–Optional

Judy Buller, Bluffton, OH

Makes 6 servings

Prep. Time: 20 minutes ❦ Cooking Time: 3–6 hours ❦ Ideal slow-cooker size: 4-qt.

Needed at Time of Preparation:

¾ cup onions, finely chopped

⅛ tsp. garlic powder

1 tsp. canola oil

½ lb. dry lentils, picked clean of stones and floaters

1 Tbsp. chili powder

2 tsp. ground cumin

1 tsp. dried oregano

2 cups fat-free, low-sodium chicken broth *use vegetable broth to keep this recipe vegetarian and/or vegan

Preparation Instructions:

1. Add all ingredients to a gallon-sized freezer bag.

2. Remove as much air as possible and seal bag.

3. Label the bag with the information below, then freeze.

Information for Freezer Bag:

LENTIL TACOS

Makes 6 servings

Cooking Time: 3–6 hours ❦ Ideal slow-cooker size: 4-qt.

Needed at Time of Cooking/ Serving:

1 cup salsa

12 taco shells *make sure yours are gluten-free to keep this recipe gluten-free

shredded lettuce, *optional*

tomatoes, chopped, *optional*

shredded, reduced-fat cheddar cheese, *optional*

fat-free sour cream, *optional*

taco sauce, *optional*

Instructions:

1. Thaw bag completely for 24–48 hours or more.

2. Empty contents of bag into crock and stir.

3. Cover. Cook on Low 3 hours for somewhat-crunchy lentils, or on Low 6 hours for soft lentils.

4. Add salsa.

5. Spoon about ¼ cup into each taco shell. Top with your choice of lettuce, tomatoes, cheese, sour cream, and taco sauce.

BBQ Veggie Joes

*10 Ing. or Fewer *Gluten-Free–Optional *Vegetarian–Optional *Vegan–Optional

Andrea Cunningham, Arlington, KS

Makes 10 servings

Prep. Time: 30 minutes ❦ Cooking Time: 8–10 hours ❦ Ideal slow-cooker size: 3-qt.

Needed at Time of Preparation:

1 cup dried lentils, rinsed and sorted

2 cups water

1½ cups chopped celery

1½ cups chopped carrots

1 cup chopped onions

¾ cup ketchup

2 Tbsp. dark brown sugar

2 Tbsp. Worcestershire sauce *choose a brand that is gluten-free, vegetarian, and/or vegan if you're making this recipe gluten-free, vegetarian, and/or vegan.

Preparation Instructions:

1. In a medium saucepan, combine lentils and water. Bring to a boil. Reduce heat. Cover and simmer 10 minutes. Let cool completely.

2. Place lentils and all remaining ingredients into a gallon-sized freezer bag.

3. Remove as much air as possible and seal bag.

4. Label bag with the information below, then freeze.

TIP: If 10 servings is just too much for you, either split the recipe between 2–3 freezer bags or make it all and freeze the leftovers into portions appropriate for your family.

Information for Freezer Bag:

BBQ VEGGIE JOES

Makes 10 servings

Cooking Time: 8–10 hours ❦ Ideal slow-cooker size: 3-qt.

Needed at Time of Cooking:

2 Tbsp. cider vinegar

10 sandwich rolls *replace with gluten-free buns if making this recipe gluten-free

Instructions:

1. Thaw bag completely for 24–48 hours or more.

2. Empty contents of freezer bag into crock.

3. Cover. Cook on Low 8–10 hours, or until lentils are soft.

4. Stir in vinegar just before serving.

5. Spoon ½ cup of lentil mixture onto each sandwich roll to serve.

SEAFOOD MAIN DISHES

Shrimp Marinara

*10 Ing. or Fewer *Gluten-Free

Jan Mast, Lancaster, PA

Makes 4–5 servings

Prep. Time: 10–15 minutes ❦ Cooking Time: 6¼–7¼ hours ❦ Ideal slow-cooker size: 4-qt.

Needed at Time of Preparation:

6-oz. can tomato paste

2 Tbsp. dried parsley

1 clove garlic, minced

¼ tsp. pepper

½ tsp. dried basil

1 tsp. dried oregano

scant ½ tsp. salt

scant ½ tsp. garlic salt

28-oz. can diced tomatoes

Preparation Instructions:

1. Add all ingredients to a gallon-sized freezer bag and smoosh around.

2. Remove as much air as possible and seal bag.

3. Label the bag with the instructions below, then freeze.

Information for Freezer Bag:

SHRIMP MARINARA

Makes 4-5 servings

Cooking Time: 6¼–7¼ hours ❦ Ideal slow-cooker size: 4-qt.

Needed at Time of Cooking/Serving:

1 lb. cooked shrimp, peeled

cooked spaghetti *replace with gluten-free pasta to keep this recipe gluten-free

grated Parmesan cheese, *optional*

Instructions:

1. Thaw bag completely for 24–48 hours or more.

2. Empty contents of freezer bag into crock.

3. Cover and cook on Low 6–7 hours.

4. Turn to slow cooker to High and add shrimp.

5. Cover and cook an additional 15–20 minutes.

6. Serve over cooked pasta and garnish with the Parmesan cheese, if using.

SHRIMP JAMBALAYA

Makes 8 servings

Cooking Time: 2¼ hours   Ideal slow-cooker size: 5-qt.

Needed at Time of Cooking/ Serving:

2 Tbsp. butter

1½ cups uncooked instant rice

1 lb. shelled, deveined, medium-sized shrimp

1 Tbsp. chopped parsley, for garnish

Instructions:

1. Thaw bag completely for 24–48 hours or more.

2. Melt butter in crock set on High. Empty freezer bag #1 into crock. Cover and cook 30 minutes.

3. Add ½ cups uncooked instant rice. Cover and cook 15 minutes.

4. Add contents of bag #2 into crock. Cover and cook on High 1 hour.

5. Add shrimp. Cook on High 30 minutes, or until liquid is absorbed.

6. Garnish with 1 Tbsp. parsley.

Shrimp Jambalaya

Gluten-Free–Optional

Karen Ashworth, Duenweg, MO

Makes 8 servings

Prep. Time: 45 minutes ❧ *Cooking Time: 2¼ hours* ❧ *Ideal slow-cooker size: 5-qt.*

Needed at Time of Preparation:

2 medium-sized onions, chopped

2 green bell peppers, chopped

3 ribs celery, chopped

1 cup chopped, cooked lean ham

2 cloves garlic, chopped

1½ cups fat-free low-sodium beef broth *use gluten-free broth to keep this recipe gluten-free

28-oz. can low-sodium chopped tomatoes

2 Tbsp. chopped parsley, fresh or dried

1 tsp. dried basil

½ tsp. dried thyme

¼ tsp. black pepper

⅓ tsp. cayenne pepper

TIP: If 8 servings is just too much for you, either split the recipe between 2 freezer bags or make it all and freeze the leftovers.

Preparation Instructions:

1. Label 2 gallon-sized freezer bags with the numbers "#1" and "#2."

2. In freezer bag #1, add the onions, bell peppers, celery, ham, and garlic. Remove as much air as possible and seal bag.

3. In bag #2, add the beef broth, chopped tomatoes, parsley, basil, thyme, black pepper, and cayenne pepper. Remove as much air as possible and seal bag.

4. Place bags #1 and #2 into a third gallon-sized freezer bag. Remove as much air as possible and seal bag.

5. Label the bag with the information opposite, then freeze.

Seafood Gumbo

Barbara Katrine Rose, Woodbridge, VA

Makes 10 servings
Prep. Time: 45 minutes ❦ *Cooking Time: 3–4 hours* ❦ *Ideal slow-cooker size: 4- to 5-qt.*

Needed at Time of Preparation:

1 lb. okra, sliced

2 Tbsp. butter

¼ cup butter, melted

¼ cup flour

1 bunch green onions, sliced

½ cup chopped celery

2 cloves garlic, minced

16-oz. can tomatoes and juice

1 bay leaf

1 Tbsp. chopped fresh parsley

1 fresh thyme sprig

1½ tsp. salt

½–1 tsp. red pepper

3–5 cups water, depending upon the consistency you like

1 lb. peeled and deveined fresh shrimp

½ lb. fresh crabmeat

Preparation Instructions:

1. Sauté okra in 2 Tbsp. butter until okra is lightly browned. Transfer to slow cooker.

2. Combine remaining butter and flour in skillet. Cook over medium heat, stirring constantly until roux is the color of chocolate, 20–25 minutes. Stir in green onions, celery, and garlic. Cook until vegetables are tender. Gently stir in remaining ingredients.

3. Add mixture into a gallon-sized freezer bag.

4. Remove as much air as possible and seal bag. Allow to cool completely.

5. Label the bag with the information below, then freeze.

TIP: If 10 servings is just too much for you, either split the recipe between 2–3 freezer bags or make it all and freeze the leftovers.

Information for Freezer Bag:

SEAFOOD GUMBO

Makes 10 servings
Cooking Time: 3–4 hours ❦ *Ideal slow-cooker size: 4- to 5-qt.*

Instructions:

1. Thaw bag completely for 24–48 hours of more.

2. Empty contents of freezer bag into crock.

3. Cover. Cook on High 3–4 hours.

Lemon Dijon Fish

*5 Ing. or Fewer *Quick to Prep *Gluten-Free–Optional

June S. Groff, Denver, PA

Makes 4 servings

Prep. Time: 10 minutes ❧ Cooking Time: 3 hours ❧ Ideal slow-cooker size: 2-qt.

Needed at Time of Preparation:

1 ½ lbs. orange roughy fillets, cut to fit in freezer bags

2 Tbsp. Dijon mustard
*make sure yours is gluten-free to keep this recipe gluten-free

3 Tbsp. butter, melted

1 tsp. Worcestershire sauce
*make sure yours is gluten-free to keep this recipe gluten-free

1 Tbsp. lemon juice

Preparation Instructions:

1. Place all ingredients into a gallon-sized freezer bag and smoosh around to coat fillets evenly.

2. Remove as much air as possible and seal bag.

3. Label the bag with the information below, then freeze.

TIP: This recipe is so easy to assemble, you may want to consider doubling all of the ingredients now and preparing 2 freezer-bag meals instead of just 1.

Information for Freezer Bag:

LEMON DIJON FISH

Makes 4 servings

Cooking Time: 3 hours ❧ Ideal slow-cooker size: 2-qt.

Instructions:

1. Thaw bag completely for 24–48 hours or more.

2. Empty contents of bag into crock and spread out evenly.

3. Cover and cook on Low 3 hours, or until fish flakes easily but is not dry or overcooked.

Spiced Cod

*10 Ing. or Fewer *Gluten-Free–Optional

Hope Comerford, Clinton Township, MI

Makes 4–6 servings

Prep. Time: 8 minutes   ❧   Cooking Time: 2 hours   ❧   Ideal slow-cooker size: 4- or 5-qt.

Needed at Time of Preparation:

4–6 cod fillets
½ cup thinly sliced red onion
1½ tsp. garlic powder
1½ tsp. onion powder
½ tsp. cumin
¼ tsp. ancho chile
1 lime, juiced
⅓ cup vegetable broth
*make sure yours is gluten-free
to keep this recipe gluten-free

Preparation Instructions:

1. Place all ingredients into a gallon-sized freezer bag and smoosh around until all fillets are well-coated.

2. Remove as much air as possible and seal bag.

3. Label the bag with the information below, then freeze.

Information for Freezer Bag:

SPICED COD

Makes 4–6 servings

Cooking Time: 2 hours ⅓Ideal slow-cooker size: 4- or 5-qt.

Instructions:

1. Thaw the bag completely for 24–48 hours or more.

2. Empty contents of bag into crock, spreading fillets out evenly.

3. Cover and cook on Low for 2 hours, or until fish flakes easily with a fork.

Herbed Flounder

*10 Ing. or Fewer *Quick to Prep *Gluten-Free

Dorothy VanDeest, Memphis, TX

Makes 6 servings

Prep. Time: 10 minutes   ❧   Cooking Time: 2–3 hours   ❧   Ideal slow-cooker size: 6-qt.

Needed at time of Preparation:

2 lbs. flounder fillets, fresh or frozen

¾ cup gluten-free, low-sodium chicken broth or stock

2 Tbsp. lemon juice

2 Tbsp. dried chives

2 Tbsp. dried minced onion

½–1 tsp. leaf marjoram

4 Tbsp. chopped fresh parsley

½ tsp. sea salt

Preparation Instructions:

1. Place all ingredients into a gallon-sized freezer bag and smoosh around until all fillets are well-coated.

2. Remove as much air as possible and seal bag.

3. Label the bag with the information below, then freeze.

Information for Freezer Bag:

HERBED FLOUNDER

Makes 6 servings

Cooking Time: 2–3 hours   ❧   Ideal slow-cooker size: 6-qt.

Instructions:

1. Thaw bag completely for 24–48 hours or more.

2. Empty contents of freezer bag into crock and spread fillets out.

3. Cover and cook on High 2–3 hours, or until fish is flaky.

Cajun Catfish

*10 Ing. or Fewer *Quick to Prep *Gluten-Free

Hope Comerford, Clinton Township, MI

Makes 4 servings

Prep. Time: 5 minutes & Cooking Time: 2 hours & Ideal slow-cooker size: 6-qt.

Needed at Time of Preparation:

4–6 oz. catfish fillets

2 tsp. paprika

1 tsp. black pepper

1 tsp. oregano

1 tsp. dried thyme

½ tsp. garlic powder

½ tsp. kosher salt

½ tsp. parsley flakes

¼ tsp. cayenne pepper

1 Tbsp. coconut oil, melted

Preparation Instructions:

1. Place all ingredients into a gallon-sized freezer bag and smoosh around to coat the fillets well.

2. Remove as much air as possible, then seal bag.

3. Label the bag with the information below, then freeze.

Information for Freezer Bag:

CAJUN CATFISH

Makes 4 servings

Cooking Time: 2 hours & Ideal slow-cooker size: 6-qt.

Needed at Time of Cooking:

1 tsp. coconut oil

Instructions:

1. Thaw bag completely for 24–48 hours or more.

2. Place coconut oil in crock and turn to High. Let it melt.

3. Empty contents of freezer bag into crock, spreading fillets out evenly.

4. Cover and cook on Low for about 2 hours, or until the fish flakes easily with a fork.

Soups, Stews & Chilis

SOUPS & STEWS

Chicken Noodle Soup

*5 Ing. or Fewer

Jennifer J. Gehman, Harrisburg, PA

Makes 6–8 servings

Prep. Time: 5–10 minutes ❧ Cooking Time: 4–8 hours ❧ Ideal slow-cooker size: 5-qt.

Needed at Time of Preparation:

2 cups uncooked cubed chicken, dark or white meat

15¼-oz. can corn, or 2 cups frozen corn

½ cup green beans

10–12 chicken bouillon cubes

3 Tbsp. bacon drippings

Preparation Instructions:

1. Place all ingredients into a gallon-sized freezer bag.

2. Remove as much air as possible and seal bag.

3. Label the bag with the information below, then freeze.

TIP: If 6–8 servings is just too much for you, either split the recipe between 2 freezer bags or make it all and freeze the leftovers.

Information for Freezer Bag:

CHICKEN NOODLE SOUP

Makes 6–8 servings

Cooking Time: 4–8 hours ❧ Ideal slow-cooker size: 5-qt

Needed at Time of Cooking:

10 cups water

½ pkg. dry kluski (or other very sturdy) noodles

½ cup peas

Instructions:

1. Thaw bag completely for 24–48 hours or more.

2. Empty contents of freezer bag into crock and pour the 10 cups of water over the top.

3. Cover. Cook on High 4–6 hours or on Low 6–8 hours.

4. Two hours before end of cooking time, stir in noodles.

5. Stir peas into slow cooker 20 minutes before end of cooking time.

Chicken and Vegetable Soup

Gluten-Free–Optional

Hope Comerford, Clinton Township, MI

Makes 4–6 servings

Prep. Time: 15 minutes 🌱 Cooking Time: 7–8 hours 🌱 Ideal slow-cooker size: 5-qt.

Needed at Time of Preparation:

1 lb. boneless skinless chicken, cut into bite-sized pieces

2 celery ribs, diced

1 small yellow squash, diced

4 oz. sliced mushrooms

2 large carrots, diced

1 medium onion, chopped

2 Tbsp. garlic powder

1 Tbsp. onion powder

1 Tbsp. basil

½ tsp. no-salt seasoning
*make sure yours is gluten-free to keep this recipe gluten-free

1 tsp. salt

black pepper to taste

32 oz. low-sodium chicken stock
*make sure yours is gluten-free to keep this recipe gluten-free

Preparation Instructions:

1. Place all ingredients into a gallon-sized freezer bag.

2. Remove as much air as possible and seal bag.

3. Label the bag with the information below, then freeze.

Information for Freezer Bag:

CHICKEN AND VEGETABLE SOUP

Makes 4–6 servings

Cooking Time: 7–8 hours 🌱 Ideal slow-cooker size: 5-qt.

Instructions:

1. Thaw bag completely for 24–48 hours or more.

2. Empty contents of bag into crock.

3. Cover and cook on Low for 7–8 hours, or until vegetables are tender.

Chicken and Vegetable Soup with Rice

Gluten-Free–Optional

Hope Comerford, Clinton Township, MI

Makes 4–6 servings

Prep. Time: 20 minutes 🌿 Cooking Time: 6½–7½ hours 🌿 Ideal slow-cooker size: 3-qt.

Needed at Time of Preparation:

1½–2 lbs. boneless, skinless chicken breasts

1½ cups chopped carrots

1½ cups chopped red onion

2 Tbsp. garlic powder

1 Tbsp. onion powder

2 tsp. salt (you can omit the salt if you're using regular stock rather than no-salt)

¼ tsp. celery seed

¼ tsp. paprika

⅛ tsp. pepper

1 dried bay leaf

8 cups no-salt chicken stock *make sure yours is gluten-free to keep this recipe gluten-free

Preparation Instructions:

1. Place all ingredients into a gallon-sized freezer bag.

2. Remove as much air as possible and seal bag.

3. Label the bag with the information below, then freeze.

Information for Freezer Bag:

CHICKEN AND VEGETABLE SOUP WITH RICE

Makes 4–6 servings

Cooking Time: 6½–7½ hours 🌿 Ideal slow-cooker size: 3-qt.

Needed at Time of Cooking/ Serving:

1 cup fresh green beans

3 cups cooked rice

Instructions:

1. Thaw bag completely for 24–48 hours or more.

2. Empty contents of the freezer bag into crock.

3. Cover and cook on Low for 6–7 hours.

4. Remove chicken and chop into bite-sized cubes. Place chicken back into crock and add in green beans. Cover and cook another 30 minutes.

5. To serve, place approximately ½ cup of the cooked rice into each bowl and ladle soup over top of the rice.

Tex-Mex Soup with Crunchy Tortillas

*10 Ing. or Fewer *Gluten-Free–Optional*

Deb Kepiro, Strasburg, PA

Makes 6 servings

Prep. Time: 10 minutes ❦ Cooking Time: 5–7 hours ❦ Ideal slow-cooker size: 3-qt.

Needed at Time of Preparation:

2 boneless, skinless chicken breasts, cubed

1 onion, chopped

1 clove garlic, crushed

14½-oz. can chopped tomatoes

4 cups chicken broth
*make sure yours is gluten-free
to keep this recipe gluten-free

¼ tsp. salt

⅛ tsp. pepper

1 mild green chile, seeded and chopped

Preparation Instructions:

1. Place all ingredients into a gallon-sized freezer bag.

2. Remove as much air as possible and seal bag.

3. Label the bag with the information below, then freeze.

Information for Freezer Bag:

TEX-MEX SOUP WITH CRUNCHY TORTILLAS

Makes 6 servings

Cooking Time: 5–7 hours ❦ Ideal slow-cooker size: 3-qt.

Needed at Time of Cooking/ Serving:

2 Tbsp. vegetable oil

4 corn tortillas, cut in half and then in ¼-inch strips *make sure yours are gluten-free to keep this recipe gluten-free

shredded Monterey Jack cheese, for serving, *optional*

chopped fresh cilantro, for serving, *optional*

Instructions:

1. Thaw bag completely for 24–48 hours or more.

2. Empty contents of freezer bag into crock.

3. Cover and cook on Low 5–7 hours.

4. Heat oil in large skillet and add tortilla strips. Cook, stirring, over medium heat until crisp. Drain strips on paper towels.

5. If desired, put 1–2 Tbsp. shredded Monterey Jack cheese in each serving bowl.

6. Ladle soup into bowls and top with tortilla strips, and fresh cilantro, if using.

Chicken Chickpea Tortilla Soup

Gluten-Free

Hope Comerford, Clinton Township, MI

Makes 4–6 servings

Prep. Time: 5 minutes ❧ Cooking Time: 6 hours ❧ Ideal slow-cooker size: 4-qt.

Needed at Time of Preparation:

2 boneless skinless chicken breasts

2 14½-oz. cans petite diced tomatoes

15-oz. can garbanzo beans (chickpeas), drained

6 cups gluten-free chicken stock

1 onion, chopped

4-oz. can diced green chiles

1 tsp. cilantro

3–4 cloves garlic, minced

1 tsp. sea salt

1 tsp. pepper

1 tsp. cumin

1 tsp. paprika

Preparation Instructions:

1. Place all ingredients into a gallon-sized freezer bag.

2. Remove as much air as possible and seal bag.

3. Label the bag with the information below, then freeze.

Information for Freezer Bag:

CHICKEN CHICKPEA TORTILLA SOUP

Makes 4–6 servings

Cooking Time: 6 hours ❧ Ideal slow-cooker size: 4-qt.

Needed at Time of Serving:

nonfat plain Greek yogurt

shredded cheddar

baked blue corn tortilla chips

Instructions:

1. Thaw bag completely for 24–48 hours or more.

2. Empty contents of freezer bag into crock.

3. Cover and cook on Low for 6 hours.

4. Remove chicken and use two forks to pull apart chicken into shreds.

5. Stir the chicken back through the soup.

6. Serve each bowl with a dollop of nonfat plain Greek yogurt, some shredded cheddar, and crushed baked blue corn tortilla chips.

Southwest Chicken and White Bean Soup

*10 Ing. or Fewer *Gluten-Free–Optional

Karen Ceneviva, Seymour, CT

Makes 6 servings

Prep. Time: 15 minutes ❦ Cooking Time: 4–10 hours ❦ Ideal slow-cooker size: 3½-qt.

Needed at Time of Preparation:

1 lb. boneless, skinless chicken breasts, cut into 1-inch cubes

1¾ cups chicken broth *choose gluten-free broth to make this recipe gluten-free

1 cup chunky salsa *choose gluten-free salsa to make this recipe gluten-free

3 cloves garlic, minced

2 Tbsp. cumin

15½-oz. can small white beans, drained and rinsed

1 cup frozen corn

1 large onion, chopped

Preparation Instructions:

1. Place all ingredients into a gallon-sized freezer bag.

2. Remove as much air as possible and seal bag.

3. Label the bag with the information below, then freeze.

Information for Freezer Bag:

SOUTHWEST CHICKEN AND WHITE BEAN SOUP

Makes 6 servings

Cooking Time: 4–10 hours ❦ Ideal slow-cooker size: 3½-qt.

Instructions:

1. Thaw bag completely for 24–48 hours or more.

2. Empty contents of freezer bag into crock.

3. Cover. Cook 8–10 hours on Low or 4–5 hours on High.

Chili Chicken Stew with Rice

*10 Ing. or Fewer *Gluten-Free

Jenny R. Unternahrer, Wayland, IA

Makes 4–5 servings

Prep. Time: 30 minutes ❦ Cooking Time: 2½–5 hours ❦ Ideal slow-cooker size: 2½-qt.

Needed at Time of Preparation:

1½ lbs. chicken tenders or boneless skinless chicken breast, sliced into strips

½ small onion, diced

15-oz. can black beans, drained (not rinsed)

14½-oz. can petite diced tomatoes, undrained

1 cup whole corn, drained if needed (thawed if frozen)

2 tsp. chili powder

½ tsp. cumin

2–4 dashes cayenne pepper

1½ tsp. salt

Preparation Instructions:

1. Place all ingredients into a gallon-sized freezer bag.

2. Remove as much air as possible and seal bag.

3. Label bag with the information below, then freeze.

Information for Freezer Bag:

CHILI CHICKEN STEW WITH RICE

Makes 4–5 servings

Cooking Time: 2½–5 hours ❦ Ideal slow-cooker size: 2½-qt.

Needed at Time of Serving:

2 cups cooked brown rice

sour cream to taste

shredded Mexican blend cheese to taste

Instructions:

1. Thaw bag completely for 24–48 hours or more.

2. Empty contents of bag into crock.

3. Cover and cook on High for 2½ hours or Low for 5 hours.

4. Shred chicken; stir to incorporate.

5. Serve over brown rice and add desired amount of sour cream and shredded Mexican blend cheese.

Easy Vegetable Beef Soup

*5 Ing. or Fewer *Quick to Prep

Bob Coffey, New Windsor, NY

Makes 15 servings

Prep. Time: 5 minutes ❦ Cooking Time: 6–8 hours ❦ Ideal slow-cooker size: 5½-qt.

Needed at Time of Preparation:

2 10-oz. cans condensed tomato soup

15-oz. can chopped tomatoes with juice

32-oz. box good-quality beef stock

1½–2 lbs. chuck roast, chopped

salt and pepper to taste

Preparation Instructions:

1. Place all ingredients into a gallon-sized freezer bag.

2. Remove as much air as possible and seal bag.

3. Label bag with the information below, then freeze.

TIP: If 15 servings is just too much for you, either split the recipe between 3–4 freezer bags or make it all and freeze the leftovers into portions appropriate for your family.

Information for Freezer Bag:

EASY VEGETABLE BEEF SOUP

Makes 15 servings

Cooking Time: 6–8 hours ❦ Ideal slow-cooker size: 5½-qt.

Needed at Time of Cooking:
16-oz. bag mixed frozen vegetables

Instructions:

1. Thaw bag completely for 24–48 hours or more.

2. Empty contents of freezer bag into crock as well as the mixed frozen vegetables.

3. Cover and cook on Low for 6–8 hours, until beef is done.

4. Season to taste with salt and pepper.

Colorful Beef Stew

Gluten-Free

Hope Comerford, Clinton Township, MI

Makes 6 servings

Prep. Time: 20 minutes   ❦   Cooking Time: 8–9 hours   ❦   Ideal slow-cooker size: 4-qt.

Needed at Time of Preparation:

2 lbs. boneless beef chuck roast, trimmed of fat and cut into ¾-inch pieces

I large red onion, chopped

2 cups gluten-free low-sodium beef broth

6-oz. can tomato paste

4 cloves garlic, minced

I Tbsp. paprika

2 tsp. dried marjoram

½ tsp. black pepper

I tsp. sea salt

I red bell pepper, sliced

I yellow bell pepper, sliced

I orange bell pepper, sliced

Preparation Instructions:

1. In a gallon-sized freezer bag, add all of the ingredients except for the bell peppers. Remove as much air as possible and seal the bag. Label this bag "#1."

2. Place the bell peppers into second gallon-sized freezer bag. Remove as much air as possible and seal the bag. Label this bag "#2."

3. Place both freezer bags into a third freezer bag. Remove as much air as possible and seal.

4. Label the bag with both freezer bags in it with the information below, then freeze.

Information for Freezer Bag:

COLORFUL BEEF STEW

Makes 6 servings

Cooking Time: 8–9 hours   ❦   Ideal slow-cooker size: 4-qt.

Instructions:

1. Thaw bag completely for 24–48 hours or more.

2. Empty contents of bag labeled "#1" into crock.

3. Cover and cook on Low for 8–9 hours.

4. The last 45 minutes of cooking time, stir in sliced bell peppers from the bag labeled "#2."

Shredded Pork Tortilla Soup

*10 Ing. or Fewer *Gluten-Free*

Hope Comerford, Clinton Township, MI

Makes 6–8 servings

Prep. Time: 10 minutes ❧ Cooking Time: 8–10 hours ❧ Ideal slow-cooker size: 5-qt.

Needed at Time of Preparation:

3 large tomatoes, chopped

1 cup chopped red onion

1 jalapeño, seeded and minced

1 lb. pork loin

2 tsp. cumin

2 tsp. chili powder

2 tsp. onion powder

2 tsp. garlic powder

2 tsp. lime juice

8 cups gluten-free chicken broth

Preparation Instructions:

1. Place all ingredients into a gallon-sized freezer bag.

2. Remove as much air as possible and seal bag.

3. Label bag with the information below, then freeze.

TIP: If 6–8 servings is just too much for you, either split the recipe between 2 freezer bags or make it all and freeze the leftovers.

Information for Freezer Bag:

SHREDDED PORK TORTILLA SOUP

Makes 6–8 servings

Cooking Time: 8–10 hours ❧ Ideal slow-cooker size: 5-qt.

Needed at Time of Serving:

fresh chopped cilantro, *optional*

tortilla chips, *optional*

avocado slices, *optional*

freshly grated Mexican cheese, *optional*

Instructions:

1. Thaw bag completely for 24–48 hours or more.

2. Empty contents of freezer bag into crock.

3. Cover and cook on Low for 8–10 hours.

4. Remove the pork and shred it between two forks. Place it back into the soup and stir.

5. Serve each bowl of soup with fresh chopped cilantro, tortilla chips, avocado slices, and freshly grated Mexican cheese, if desired . . . or any other garnishes you would like!

Pork Thai Stew

*10 Ing. or Fewer *Gluten-Free–Optional

Marilyn Mowry, Irving, TX

Makes 6 servings

Prep. Time: 15–30 minutes ❧ Cooking Time: 2½–3 hours ❧ Ideal slow-cooker size: 4-qt.

Needed at Time of Preparation:

2 lbs. pork tenderloin,
cut into 1½-inch cubes

2 cloves garlic, sliced

2 cups sliced red bell pepper

¼ cup rice vinegar

½ cup teriyaki sauce *make
sure yours is gluten-free to
make this recipe gluten-free

1–2 tsp. red pepper flakes,
according to your taste preference

Preparation Instructions:

1. Place all ingredients into a gallon-sized freezer bag.

2. Remove as much air as possible and seal bag.

3. Label bag with the information below, then freeze.

Information for Freezer Bag:

PORK THAI STEW

Makes 6 servings

Cooking Time: 2½–3 hours ❧ Ideal slow-cooker size: 4-qt.

Needed at Time of Cooking/ Serving:

¼–½ cup creamy peanut butter

cooked rice

chopped peanuts, *optional*

chopped green onions, *optional*

Instructions:

1. Thaw bag completely for 24–48 hours.

2. Grease interior of slow-cooker crock.

3. Empty contents of freezer bag into crock.

4. Cover and cook on Low 2–2½ hours, or until meat is tender.

5. Remove pork cubes and shred meat with 2 forks, the place back in stew.

6. Stir in peanut butter. Cover and continue cooking for 30 more minutes, until heated through.

7. Serve over cooked rice.

8. Pass bowls of chopped peanuts and sliced green onions for each diner to add as they wish.

Kielbasa Soup

*10 Ing. or Fewer *Gluten-Free–Optional

Janie Steele, Moore, OK

Makes 6–8 servings

Prep. Time: 20 minutes 💥 Cooking Time: 5 hours 💥 Ideal slow-cooker size: 4-qt.

Needed at Time of Preparation:

1 lb. kielbasa, sliced thin
*choose gluten-free kielbasa
to make this recipe gluten-free

8 cups chicken broth
*choose gluten-free broth to
make this recipe gluten-free

2 14-oz. cans cannellini beans with juice

1 onion, diced

1 bay leaf

1 tsp. dried thyme

¼ tsp. red pepper flakes

Preparation Instructions:

1. In skillet, brown kielbasa slices over high heat until some edges are brown. If you don't have time you can skip this step.

2. Add the kielbasa and remaining ingredients to a gallon-sized freezer bag.

3. Remove as much air as possible and seal the bag. Let it cool.

4. Label the bag with the information below, then freeze.

TIP: If 6–8 servings is just too much for you, either split the recipe between 2 freezer bags or make it all and freeze the leftovers.

Information for Freezer Bag:

KIELBASA SOUP

Makes 6–8 servings

Cooking Time: 5 hours 💥 Ideal slow-cooker size: 4-qt.

Needed at Time of Cooking:

8 oz. rainbow rotini, uncooked *replace with gluten-free pasta to make this recipe gluten-free

3 cloves garlic, minced

1 lb. chopped fresh spinach

salt and pepper to taste

Instructions:

1. Thaw bag completely for 24–48 hours or more.

2. Empty contents of freezer bag into crock.

3. Cover and cook on Low for 4 hours.

4. Add rotini and garlic. Cook an additional hour on Low, or until pasta is as tender as you like it.

5. Stir in chopped spinach. Add salt and pepper to taste. Remove bay leaf.

Quick Kielbasa Soup

*5 Ing. or Fewer *Quick to Prep *Gluten-Free–Optional*

Bernice M. Gnidovec, Streator, IL

Makes 8 servings

Prep. Time: 10 minutes ❧ Cooking Time: 12 hours ❧ Ideal slow-cooker size: 8-qt.

Needed at Time of Preparation:

16-oz. pkg. frozen mixed vegetables, or your choice of vegetables

6-oz. can tomato paste

1 medium onion, chopped

1½ lbs. kielbasa, cut into ¼-inch pieces
*make sure yours is gluten-free to keep this recipe gluten-free

Preparation Instructions:

1. Place all ingredients into a gallon-sized freezer bag.

2. Remove as much air as possible and seal bag.

3. Label bag with the information below, then freeze.

TIP: If 8 servings is just too much for you, either split the recipe between 2 freezer bags or make it all and freeze the leftovers.

Information for Freezer Bag:

QUICK KIELBASA SOUP

Makes 8 servings

Cooking Time: 12 hours ❧ Ideal slow-cooker size: 8-qt.

Needed at Time of Cooking:

3 medium potatoes, diced

4-qt. (16 cups) water

Instructions:

1. Thaw bag completely for 24–48 hours or more.

2. Empty contents of freezer bag into crock along with the diced potatoes and 4 quarts of water.

3. Cover. Cook on Low 12 hours.

Shepherd Stew

*10 Ing. or Fewer *Gluten-Free

Mary Stoltzfus, Manheim, PA

Makes 8–10 servings

Prep. Time: 15 minutes ❧ Cooking Time: 5–8 hours ❧ Ideal slow-cooker size: 5- to 6-qt.

Needed at Time of Preparation

1 ½ lbs. lentils, uncooked

1 ½ celery ribs, chopped

2 large carrots, peeled and grated

1 cup chopped onion

1 bay leaf

½ tsp. thyme

¼ tsp. crushed red pepper

1–1 ½ tsp. salt

2 ham hocks

2 cups water

Preparation Instructions:

1. Combine all ingredients in a gallon-sized freezer bag.

2. Remove as much air as possible and seal bag.

3. Label bag with the information below, then freeze.

TIP: If 8–10 servings is just too much for you, either split the recipe between 2 freezer bags or make it all and freeze the leftovers into portions appropriate for your family.

Information for Freezer Bag:

SHEPHERD STEW

Makes 8–10 servings

Cooking Time: 5–8 hours ❧ Ideal slow-cooker size: 5- to 6-qt.

Needed at Time of Cooking/ Serving:

8 cups water

pita bread *replace with gluten-free pita to keep this recipe gluten-free

Instructions:

1. Thaw bag completely for 24–48 hours or more.

2. Combine contents of freezer bag with additional 8 cups water in crock.

3. Cover and cook on Low 5–8 hours.

4. Remove bay leaf.

5. Serve with pita bread.

The Best Bean and Ham Soup

Gluten-Free

Hope Comerford, Clinton Township, MI

Makes 8–10 servings

Prep. Time: 8 minutes ❦ Soaking Time: 8 hours or overnight
Cooking Time: 8–12 hours ❦ Ideal slow-cooker size: 7-qt.

Needed at Time of Preparation:

1 lb. dry navy beans, soaked 8 hours or
overnight, drained and rinsed

1 meaty ham bone or shank

1 cup chopped onions

2 cloves garlic, minced

1 cup chopped celery

1 cup mashed potato flakes

¼ cup chopped parsley

1 Tbsp. salt

1 tsp. pepper

1 tsp. nutmeg

1 tsp. oregano

1 tsp. basil

1 bay leaf

2 cups water

Preparation Instructions:

1. Place all ingredients into a gallon-sized freezer bag.

2. Remove as much air as possible and seal bag.

3. Label bag with the information below, then freeze.

TIP: If 8–10 servings is just too much for you, make the whole recipe and freeze the leftovers into portions appropriate for your family.

Information for Freezer Bag:

THE BEST BEAN AND HAM SOUP

Makes 8–10 servings

Cooking Time: 8–12 hours ❦ Ideal slow-cooker size: 7-qt.

Needed at Time of Cooking:

12 cups water

Instructions:

1. Thaw bag completely for 24–48 hours or more.

2. Empty contents of bag into crock and add the additional 12 cups of water, enough to completely cover the ham bone.

3. Cover and cook on Low for 8–12 hours.

4. Remove ham bone and any gristle pieces and cut up any large chunks of ham. Stir back through soup.

Slow-Cooker Bean Soup

*10 Ing. or Fewer *Gluten-Free–Optional*

Lois Ostrander, Lebanon, PA

Makes 8 servings

Prep. Time: 20 minutes ❧ Cooking Time: 5½ hours ❧ Ideal slow-cooker size: 3-qt.

Needed at Time of Preparation:

1 ham hock

40½-oz. can great northern beans, rinsed and drained

1 medium onion, chopped

1 carrot, chopped

4–5 medium-sized potatoes, chopped

2 Tbsp. Mrs. Dash Original Seasoning Blend

32-oz. box chicken broth
*make sure yours is gluten-free to keep this recipe gluten-free

Preparation Instructions:

1. Place all ingredients into a gallon-sized freezer bag.

2. Remove as much air as possible and seal bag.

3. Label bag with the information below, then freeze.

TIP: If 8 servings is just too much for you, make the whole recipe and freeze the leftovers.

Information for Freezer Bag:

SLOW-COOKER BEAN SOUP

Makes 8 servings

Cooking Time: 5½ hours ❧ Ideal slow-cooker size: 3-qt.

Instructions:

1. Thaw bag completely for 24–48 hours or more.

2. Empty contents of freezer bag into crock. Add either more chicken broth or water to make sure ham hock is completely covered.

3. Cook on High for 3 hours, then turn down to Low for 2 hours.

4. Take out ham hock. Remove ham from bone, and chop ham into bite-sized pieces.

5. Return ham to slow cooker. Cook on Low an additional 30 minutes.

Split Pea Soup

*10 Ing. or Fewer *Gluten-Free

Phyllis Good, Lancaster, PA

Makes 8–10 servings

Prep. Time: 20 minutes ❧ Cooking Time: 4–8 hours ❧ Ideal slow-cooker size: 6-qt.

Needed at Time of Preparation:

3 cups dried split peas
(a little over 1 pound)

2 cups water

½ tsp. garlic powder

½ tsp. dried oregano

1 cup of diced, or thinly sliced, carrots

1 cup chopped celery

1 tsp. salt

¼–½ tsp. pepper
(coarsely ground is great)

1 ham shank or hock

Preparation Instructions:

1. Place all ingredients into a gallon-sized freezer bag.

2. Remove as much air as possible and seal bag.

3. Label bag with the information below, then freeze.

TIP: If 8–10 servings is just too much for you, make the whole recipe and freeze the leftovers into portions appropriate for your family.

Information for Freezer Bag:

SPLIT PEA SOUP

Makes 8–10 servings

Cooking Time: 4–8 hours ❧ Ideal slow-cooker size: 6-qt.

Needed at Time of Cooking:

10 cups water

Instructions:

1. Thaw bag completely for 24–48 hours.

2. Empty contents of freezer bag into crock and pour in the additional 10 cups of water.

3. Cover. Cook on Low 4–8 hours, or until ham is tender and falling off the bone, and the peas are very soft.

4. Use a slotted spoon to lift the ham bone out of the soup. Allow it to cool until you can handle it without burning yourself.

5. Cut the ham into bite-sized pieces. Stir it back into the soup.

6. Heat the soup for 10 minutes, and then serve.

Vegetable Soup Galore

*Gluten-Free–Optional *Vegetarian *Vegan*

Janice Muller, Derwood, MD

Makes 10 servings

Prep. Time: 20 minutes   ❧   Cooking Time: 4½–5½ hours   ❧   Ideal slow-cooker size: 6-qt.

Needed at Time of Preparation:

12-oz. can whole tomatoes

1 cup thinly sliced carrots

1 cup chopped onions

12-oz. bag frozen peas

12-oz. bag frozen corn

16-oz. bag frozen lima beans

4 vegetable bouillon cubes *make sure yours are gluten-free to keep this recipe gluten-free

1 Tbsp. salt

¼ tsp. pepper

½ tsp. dried basil

1 bay leaf

¼ tsp. dill seed

3½ cups water

Preparation Instructions:

1. Place all ingredients into a gallon-sized freezer bag.

2. Remove as much air as possible and seal bag.

3. Label bag with the information below, then freeze.

TIP: If 10 servings is just too much for you, either split the recipe between 2 freezer bags or make it all and freeze the leftovers into portions appropriate for your family.

Information for Freezer Bag:

VEGETABLE SOUP GALORE

Makes 10 servings

Cooking Time: 4½–5½ hours   ❧   Ideal slow-cooker size: 6-qt.

Needed at Time of Cooking:

1 cup diced raw potatoes

4 cups water, *divided*

2 Tbsp. cornstarch

Instructions:

1. Thaw bag completely for 24–48 hours or more.

2. Empty contents of freezer bag into crock along with the diced potatoes and additional 3½ cups water.

3. Cover and cook on Low for 4–5 hours, until vegetables are tender.

4. Mix cornstarch and ½ cup water until smooth.

5. Whisk mixture into hot soup and cook for an additional 30 minutes until thickened. Stir before serving.

Lentil Spinach Soup

*10 Ing. or Fewer *Gluten-Free *Vegetarian *Vegan

Marilyn Widrick, Adams, NY

Makes 4–6 servings

Prep. Time: 20 minutes ❦ Cooking Time: 2½ hours ❦ Ideal slow-cooker size: 5-qt.

Needed at Time of Preparation:

1 Tbsp. olive oil

4 medium carrots, chopped

1 small onion, diced

1 tsp. ground cumin

14½-oz. can diced tomatoes

14½-oz. can gluten-free vegetable broth

1 cup dry lentils

2 cups water

¼ tsp. salt

⅛ tsp. pepper

Preparation Instructions:

1. Heat olive oil in cooking pot. Add carrots and onion. Cook 8–10 minutes over medium heat.

2. Place the carrot and onion mixture as well as the remaining ingredients into a gallon-sized freezer bag.

3. Remove as much air as possible and seal bag. Let cool completely.

4. Label the bag with the information below, then freeze.

Information for Freezer Bag:

LENTIL SPINACH SOUP

Makes 4–6 servings

Cooking Time: 2½ hours ❦ Ideal slow-cooker size: 5-qt.

Needed at Time of Cooking:

5-oz. bag fresh spinach, chopped

Instructions:

1. Thaw bag completely for 24–48 hours or more.

2. Empty contents of freezer bag into crock.

3. Cover and cook on Low 2 hours.

4. Add spinach. Cook on Low an additional 15–25 minutes.

Savory Lentil Soup

*Gluten-Free–Optional *Vegetarian–Optional *Vegan–Optional*

Margaret W. High, Lancaster, PA

Makes 6 servings

Prep. Time: 15 minutes 🌱 Cooking Time: 5 hours 🌱 Ideal slow-cooker size: 4-qt.

Needed at Time of Preparation:

1½ cups dry lentils

4 cups beef stock *replace with vegetable stock to make this recipe vegetarian/vegan

*replace with gluten-free beef stock to make this recipe gluten-free

½ cup red wine

1 onion, chopped

2 carrots, diced

2 Tbsp. olive oil

1 bay leaf

1 tsp. salt

¼ tsp. freshly ground pepper

1½ tsp. dried oregano

½ tsp. cumin

½ cup tomato sauce or 1 Tbsp. tomato paste

3 Tbsp. red wine vinegar

½ cup sliced black olives

2 cloves garlic, minced

Preparation Instructions:

1. In a gallon-sized freezer bag, add the lentils, beef stock, red wine, onion, carrots, olive oil, bay leaf, salt, pepper, oregano, and cumin. Remove as much air as possible and seal the bag. Label this bag "#1."

2. In a sandwich-sized ziplock bag, add the tomato sauce, red wine vinegar, black olives, and garlic. Remove as much air as possible and seal the bag. Label this bag "#2."

3. Place both bags into a third gallon-sized freezer bag, remove as much air as possible and seal the bag.

4. Label the bag with the information below, then freeze.

Information for Freezer Bag:

SAVORY LENTIL SOUP

Makes 6 servings

Cooking Time: 5 hours 🌱 Ideal slow-cooker size: 4-qt.

Needed at Time of Cooking:

1½ cups water

½ cup chopped fresh parsley

Instructions:

1. Thaw bag completely for 24–48 hours or more.
2. Empty contents of bag #1 into crock along with the water.
3. Cover and cook on Low 4 hours.
4. Add contents of bag #2 and the fresh parsley. Stir. Cook on Low 1 more hour.

Fresh Tomato Soup

*10 Ing. or Fewer *Gluten-Free *Vegetarian–Optional *Vegan–Optional

Rebecca Plank Leichty, Harrisonburg, VA

Makes 6 servings

Prep. Time: 20–25 minutes 🌿 *Cooking Time: 3–4 hours* 🌿 *Ideal slow-cooker size: 3½- to 4-qt.*

Needed at Time of Preparation:

5 cups diced ripe tomatoes (your choice about whether or not to peel them)

1 Tbsp. tomato paste

4 cups salt-free chicken broth *replace with vegetable broth to make this vegetarian/vegan

*choose gluten-free broth to make this recipe gluten-free

1 carrot, grated

1 onion, minced

1 Tbsp. minced garlic

1 tsp. dried basil

Pepper, to taste

2 Tbsp. lemon juice

1 dried bay leaf

Preparation Instructions:

1. Place all ingredients into a gallon-sized freezer bag.

2. Remove as much air as possible and seal bag.

3. Label bag with the information below, then freeze.

Information for Freezer Bag:

FRESH TOMATO SOUP

Makes 6 servings

Cooking Time: 3–4 hours 🌿 *Ideal slow-cooker size: 3½- to 4-qt.*

Instructions:

1. Thaw bag completely for 24–48 hours or more.

2. Empty contents of freezer bag into crock.

3. Cook on Low for 3–4 hours. Stir once while cooking.

4. Remove bay leaf before serving.

Tomato Basil Soup

*10 Ing. or Fewer *Gluten-Free–Optional *Vegetarian*

Janet Melvin, Cincinnati, OH

Makes 12 servings

Prep. Time: 15 minutes   ❧   Cooking Time: 3½ hours   ❧   Ideal slow-cooker size: 4-qt.

Needed at Time of Preparation:

½ cup very finely diced onion

2 cloves garlic, minced

2 cups vegetable stock
*choose gluten-free stock to keep this recipe gluten-free

2 28-oz. cans crushed tomatoes

1 Tbsp. salt

½ tsp. pepper

Preparation Instructions:

1. Place all ingredients into a gallon-sized freezer bag.

2. Remove as much air as possible and seal bag.

3. Label bag with the information below, then freeze.

TIP: If 12 servings is just too much for you, either split the recipe between 2 freezer bags or make it all and freeze the leftovers into portions appropriate for your family.

Information for Freezer Bag:

TOMATO BASIL SOUP

Makes 12 servings

Cooking Time: 3½ hours   ❧   Ideal slow-cooker size: 4-qt.

Needed at time of Cooking:

¼ cup chopped fresh basil, plus more for garnish

1 cup heavy cream, room temperature

Instructions:

1. Thaw bag completely for 24–48 hours or more.

2. Empty contents of freezer bag into crock. Add the ¼ cup chopped fresh basil.

3. Cover and cook on High for 3 hours. You may puree soup at this point if you wish for a totally smooth soup.

4. Stir in heavy cream and cook an additional 30 minutes on Low.

5. Garnish each serving with a few ribbons of fresh basil.

French Onion Soup

*5 Ing. or Fewer *Gluten-Free–Optional*

Hope Comerford, Clinton Township, MI

Makes 6–8 servings

Prep. Time: 10 minutes ❧ Cooking Time: 7–8 hours ❧ Ideal slow-cooker size: 5-qt.

Needed at Time of Preparation:

3–4 large sweet yellow onions, sliced thinly

½ tsp. pepper

1 bay leaf

7 cups beef stock *choose gluten-free stock to keep this recipe gluten-free

1 cup dry white wine (such as a chardonnay)

Preparation Instructions:

1. Place all ingredients into a gallon-sized freezer bag.

2. Remove as much air as possible and seal bag.

3. Label bag with the information below, then freeze.

TIP: If 6–8 servings is just too much for you, either split the recipe between 2 freezer bags or make it all and freeze the leftovers.

Information for Freezer Bag:

FRENCH ONION SOUP

Makes 6–8 servings

Cooking Time: 7–8 hours ❧ Ideal slow-cooker size: 5-qt.

Needed at Time of Cooking/Serving:

2 sprigs fresh thyme

loaf of French bread, sliced *omit bread or use gluten-free bread to keep this recipe gluten-free

4 oz. Gruyère cheese, sliced thinly

Instructions:

1. Thaw bag completely for 24–48 hours or more.

2. Empty contents of freezer bag into crock along with the 2 sprigs of fresh thyme.

3. Cover and cook on Low for 7–8 hours. Remove the thyme sprigs and bay leaf.

4. Serve each bowl of soup in an oven-safe bowl and place a slice of bread on top, topped with enough cheese to cover the entire top. Place it in the oven under the broiler for a few minutes, or until the cheese starts to bubble.

Broccoli Cheese Soup

10 Ing. or Fewer

Hope Comerford, Clinton Township, MI

Makes 6 servings

Prep. Time: 15 minutes ❦ Cooking Time: 6–7 hours ❦ Ideal slow-cooker size: 3-qt.

Needed at Time of Preparation:

1 head broccoli,
chopped into tiny pieces

1 onion, chopped finely

10¾-oz. can condensed cheddar
cheese soup

3 cups water

4 chicken bouillon cubes

1½ tsp. garlic powder

1 tsp. onion powder

½ tsp. seasoned salt

1 tsp. pepper

Preparation Instructions:

1. Place all ingredients into a gallon-sized freezer bag.

2. Remove as much air as possible and seal bag.

3. Label bag with the information below, then freeze.

Information for Freezer Bag:

BROCCOLI CHEESE SOUP

Makes 6 servings

Cooking Time: 6–7 hours ❦ Ideal slow-cooker size: 3-qt.

Needed at Time of Cooking:

2 12-oz. cans evaporated milk

16-oz. block Velveeta cheese,
chopped into pieces

Instructions:

1. Thaw bag completely for 24–48 hours or more.

2. Empty contents of freezer bag into crock along with the evaporated milk.

3. Cover and cook on Low for 6–7 hours.

4. About 5–10 minutes before eating, turn slow cooker to High and stir in Velveeta cheese until melted.

Creamy Butternut Squash Soup

*10 Ing. or Fewer *Gluten-Free *Vegetarian–Optional *Vegan–Optional

Hope Comerford, Clinton Township, MI

Makes 4–6 servings

Prep. Time: 20 minutes ❧ Cooking Time: 8 hours ❧ Ideal slow-cooker size: 3-qt.

Needed at Time of Preparation:

1½ lbs. butternut squash, peeled and cut into 1-inch chunks

1 small onion, quartered

1 carrot, cut into 1-inch chunks

¼ tsp. cinnamon

⅓ tsp. nutmeg

½ tsp. sugar

¼ tsp. salt

⅓ tsp. pepper

⅓ tsp. ginger

3 cups gluten-free chicken or vegetable stock

Preparation Instructions:

1. Place all ingredients into a gallon-sized freezer bag.

2. Remove as much air as possible and seal bag.

3. Label bag with the information below, then freeze.

Information for Freezer Bag:

CREAMY BUTTERNUT SQUASH SOUP

Makes 4–6 servings

Cooking Time: 8 hours ❧ Ideal slow-cooker size: 3-qt.

Needed at Time of Cooking:

1 small sweet potato, cut into 1-inch chunks

1 cup heavy cream or half-and-half *sub for vegan

Instructions:

1. Thaw bag completely for 24–48 hours or more.

2. Empty the contents of the freezer bag into the crock along with the sweet potato chunks.

3. Cover and cook on Low for 8 hours, or until the vegetables are soft.

4. Using an immersion blender, blend the soup until smooth.

5. Remove ¼ cup of the soup and mix it with the 1 cup of heavy cream or half-and-half. Pour this into the crock and mix until well combined.

Enchilada Soup

*10 Ing. or Fewer *Gluten-Free–Optional *Vegetarian *Vegan

Melissa Paskvan, Novi, MI

Makes 6–8 servings

Prep. Time: 5 minutes ❦ Cooking Time: 6–8 hours ❦ Ideal slow-cooker size: 6-qt.

Needed at Time of Preparation:

14½-oz. can of diced tomatoes
with green chiles or chipotles

12-oz. jar enchilada sauce

4 cups vegetable broth
*choose gluten-free broth to
make this recipe gluten-free

1 small onion, chopped

3 cups tricolored peppers, sliced

10-oz. pkg. frozen corn

1 cup water

Preparation Instructions:

1. Place all ingredients into a gallon-sized freezer bag.

2. Remove as much air as possible and seal bag.

3. Label bag with the information below, then freeze.

TIP: If 6–8 servings is just too much for you, either split the recipe between 2 freezer bags or make it all and freeze the leftovers.

Information for Freezer Bag:

ENCHILADA SOUP

Makes 6–8 servings

Cooking Time: 6–8 hours ❦ Ideal slow-cooker size: 6-qt.

Needed at Time of Cooking:

½ cup uncooked quinoa

Instructions:

1. Thaw bag completely for 24–48 hours or more.

2. Empty contents of bag into crock along with the quinoa.

3. Cover and cook on Low for 6–8 hours.

Gumbo

Gluten-Free–Optional

Dorothy Ealy, Los Angeles, CA

Makes 8 servings

Prep. Time: 30 minutes ❧ Cooking Time: 4¼–5½ hours ❧ Ideal slow-cooker size: 5-qt.

Needed at Time of Preparation:

2 onions, chopped

3 ribs celery, chopped

½ cup diced green bell pepper

2 cloves garlic, chopped

1 cup chopped fresh or frozen okra

½ cup diced andouille or chorizo sausage *make sure yours is gluten-free to keep this recipe gluten-free

2 15-oz. cans tomatoes, undrained

3 Tbsp. tomato paste

1 chicken bouillon cube *choose gluten-free cubes to make this recipe gluten-free

¼ tsp. freshly ground black pepper

¼ tsp. dried thyme

Preparation Instructions:

1. Place all ingredients into a gallon-sized freezer bag.

2. Remove as much air as possible and seal bag.

3. Label bag with the information below, then freeze.

TIP: If 8 servings is just too much for you, either split the recipe between 2 freezer bags or make it all and freeze the leftovers.

Information for Freezer Bag:

GUMBO

Makes 8 servings

Cooking Time: 4¼–5½ hours ❧ Ideal slow-cooker size: 5-qt.

Needed at Time of Cooking:

1½ lbs. raw shrimp, peeled and deveined, chopped if large

Serving Suggestion: Serve over rice, or serve with French bread. *omit French bread to keep this recipe gluten-free

Instructions:

1. Thaw bag completely for 24–48 hours or more.

2. Empty contents of freezer bag into crock.

3. Cover and cook on Low for 4–5 hours, until vegetables are soft.

4. Add shrimp. Cook for 15–20 more minutes on Low, until shrimp are just opaque and cooked through. Thin Gumbo if necessary with a little water, broth, or wine. Taste and adjust salt.

CHILIS

Chicken Chili

*10 Ing. or Fewer *Gluten-Free

Sharon Miller, Holmesville, OH

Makes 6 servings

Prep. Time: 15 minutes   Cooking Time: 5–6 hours   Ideal slow-cooker size: 4-qt.

Needed at Time of Preparation:

2 lbs. boneless, skinless chicken breasts, cubed

2 Tbsp. butter

2 14-oz. cans diced tomatoes, undrained

15-oz. can red kidney beans, rinsed and drained

1 cup diced onion

1 cup diced red bell pepper

1–2 Tbsp. chili powder, according to your taste preference

1 tsp. cumin

1 tsp. dried oregano

Salt and pepper, to taste

Preparation Instructions:

1. In skillet on high heat, brown chicken cubes in butter until they have some browned edges.

2. Place chicken as well as the rest of the ingredients into a gallon-sized freezer bag.

3. Remove as much air as possible and seal. Let cool.

4. Label bag with information below, then freeze.

Information for Freezer Bag:

CHICKEN CHILI

Makes 6 servings

Cooking Time: 5–6 hours   Ideal slow-cooker size: 4-qt.

Serving Suggestion: This goes well with shredded cheddar cheese and sour cream on top.

Instructions:

1. Thaw bag completely for 24–48 hours or more.

2. Empty contents of freezer bag into crock.

3. Cover and cook on Low for 5–6 hours.

Chipotle Chili

*10 Ing. or Fewer *Gluten-Free

Janie Steele, Moore, OK

Makes 6–8 servings

Prep. Time: 30 minutes ❧ Cooking Time: 3–6 hours ❧ Ideal slow-cooker size: 3- to 4-qt.

Needed at Time of Preparation:

1¼ lbs. boneless, skinless chicken thighs, cubed

2 cloves garlic, chopped

1 lb. butternut squash, peeled and cubed

15-oz. can pinto beans, rinsed and drained

juice and zest of ½ an orange

2–3 chipotle peppers in adobo sauce, minced

2 Tbsp. tomato paste

Preparation Instructions:

1. In skillet on high heat, brown chicken cubes in butter until they have some browned edges.

2. Place chicken as well as the rest of the ingredients into a gallon-sized freezer bag.

3. Remove as much air as possible and seal. Let cool.

4. Label bag with information below, then freeze.

TIP: If 6–8 servings is just too much for you, either split the recipe between 2 freezer bags or make it all and freeze the leftovers.

Information for Freezer Bag:

CHIPOTLE CHILI

Makes 6–8 servings

Cooking Time: 3–6 hours ❧ Ideal slow-cooker size: 3- to 4-qt.

Needed at Time of Cooking:

2 green onions, sliced

chopped cilantro, *optional*

Instructions:

1. Thaw bag completely for 24–48 hours or more.

2. Empty contents of freezer bag into crock.

3. Cover and cook 3–4 hours on High or 5–6 hours on Low, until chicken is done.

4. Mash some of the stew with potato masher to make it thicker.

5. Stir in green onions and cilantro, if using. Serve hot.

White Chili

Gluten-Free–Optional

Rebecca Plank Leichty, Harrisonburg, VA

Makes 6–8 servings

Prep. Time: 15 minutes   Cooking Time: 4–10 hours   Ideal slow-cooker size: 5-qt.

Needed at Time of Preparation:

15-oz. can garbanzo beans (chickpeas), undrained

15-oz. can navy beans, undrained

15-oz. can pinto beans, undrained

1-qt. frozen corn, or 2 1-lb. bags frozen corn

1½ cups shredded cooked chicken

2 Tbsp. minced onions

1 red bell pepper, diced

3 tsp. minced garlic

3 tsp. ground cumin

½ tsp. salt

½ tsp. dried oregano

2 15-oz. cans chicken broth
*choose gluten-free broth to make this recipe gluten-free

Preparation Instructions:

1. Place all ingredients into a gallon-sized freezer bag.

2. Remove as much air as possible and seal bag.

3. Label bag with the information below, then freeze.

TIP: If 6–8 servings is just too much for you, either split the recipe between 2 freezer bags or make it all and freeze the leftovers.

Information for Freezer Bag:

WHITE CHILI

Makes 6–8 servings

Cooking Time: 4–10 hours   Ideal slow-cooker size: 5-qt.

Instructions:

1. Thaw bag completely for 24–48 hours or more.

2. Empty contents of freezer bag into crock.

3. Cover. Cook on Low 8–10 hours or on High 4–5 hours.

White Bean and Chicken Chili
*Gluten-Free

Hope Comerford, Clinton Township, MI

Makes 6–8 servings

Prep. Time: 15 minutes 🌱 Cooking Time: 8–10 hours 🌱 Ideal slow-cooker size: 5-qt.

Needed at Time of Preparation:

2 lbs. boneless, skinless chicken, cut into bite-sized chunks

½ cup dry navy beans, soaked overnight, drained, and rinsed

½ cup dry great northern beans, soaked overnight, drained, and rinsed

½ cup chopped carrots

1½ cups chopped onion

14½-oz. can petite diced tomatoes

10-oz. can diced tomatoes with lime juice and cilantro

5 cloves garlic, minced

6-oz. can tomato paste

1 Tbsp. cumin

1 Tbsp. chili powder

1 tsp. salt

¼ tsp. pepper

8 tsp. Massel chicken bouillon seasoning granules

Preparation Instructions:

1. Place all ingredients into a gallon-sized freezer bag.

2. Remove as much air as possible and seal bag.

3. Label bag with the information below, then freeze.

TIP: If 6–8 servings is just too much for you, either split the recipe between 2 freezer bags or make it all and freeze the leftovers.

Information for Freezer Bag:

WHITE BEAN AND CHICKEN CHILI

Makes 6–8 servings

Cooking Time: 8–10 hours 🌱 Ideal slow-cooker size: 5-qt.

Needed at Time of Cooking:

8 cups water

Instructions:

1. Thaw bag completely for 24–48 hours or more.

2. Empty contents of freezer bag and 8 cups of water into crock.

3. Cover and cook on Low for 8–10 hours.

No-Beans Chili

Gluten-Free–Optional

Sharon Timpe, Jackson, WI

Makes 10–12 servings

Prep. Time: 35 minutes ❧ Cooking Time: 6–10 hours ❧ Ideal slow-cooker size: 5- or 6-qt.

Needed at Time of Preparation:

2–3 Tbsp. oil

1½ lbs. round steak, cubed

1½ lbs. chuck steak, cubed

1 cup red wine

1½ tsp. dried oregano

2 tsp. dried parsley

1 medium onion, chopped

1 cup chopped celery

1 cup chopped carrots

28-oz. can stewed tomatoes

8-oz. can tomato sauce

1 cup beef broth *choose gluten-free broth to keep this recipe gluten-free

1 Tbsp. vinegar

1 Tbsp. brown sugar

2 Tbsp. chili powder

1 tsp. cumin

¼ tsp. pepper

1 tsp. salt

Preparation Instructions:

1. Heat oil in a skillet and brown the beef cubes. You may have to do this in two batches.

2. Place the browned beef cubes and all remaining ingredients into a gallon-sized freezer bag.

3. Remove as much air as possible and seal bag. Let cool.

4. Label bag with the information below, then freeze.

TIP: If 10–12 servings is just too much for you, either split the recipe between 2–3 freezer bags or make it all and freeze the leftovers into portions appropriate for your family.

Information for Freezer Bag:

NO-BEANS CHILI

Makes 10–12 servings

Cooking Time: 6–10 hours ❧ Ideal slow-cooker size: 5- or 6-qt.

Instructions:

1. Thaw bag completely for 24–48 hours or more.

2. Empty contents of freezer bag into crock.

3. Cook on Low 9–10 hours or High 6–7 hours, until meat is very tender.

Chili in a Slow Cooker

*10 Ing. or Fewer *Gluten-Free

Jo Zimmerman, Lebanon, PA

Makes 6 servings

Prep. Time: 15 minutes ❦ Cooking Time: 6 hours ❦ Ideal slow-cooker size: 5-qt.

Needed at Time of Preparation:

1½ lbs. ground beef

1 medium onion, chopped

1 green pepper, chopped

½ tsp. garlic powder

14½-oz. can of diced tomatoes

2 5½-oz. cans V8 juice

1 Tbsp. chili powder

Pinch of red pepper flakes

Preparation Instructions:

1. Place all ingredients into a gallon-sized ziplock bag, crumbling the beef as you put it in.

2. Remove as much air as possible and seal bag.

3. Label the bag with the information below, then freeze.

Information for Freezer Bag:

CHILI IN A SLOW COOKER

Makes 6 servings

Cooking Time: 6 hours ❦ Ideal slow-cooker size: 5-qt.

Serving Suggestion: This pairs well with cornbread.

Instructions:

1. Thaw bag completely for 24–48 hours or more.

2. Empty contents of freezer bag into crock and stir, breaking the ground beef apart a bit.

3. Cover and cook on Low for 6 hours.

Metric Equivalent Measurements

dash = little less than ⅛ tsp.

3 tsp. = 1 Tbsp.

2 Tbsp. = 1 oz.

4 Tbsp. = ¼ cup

5 Tbsp. plus 1 tsp. = ⅓ cup

8 Tbsp. = ½ cup

12 Tbsp. = ¾ cup

16 Tbsp. = 1 cup

1 cup = 8 oz. liquid

2 cups = 1 pt.

4 cups = 1 qt.

4 qt. = 1 gal.

1 stick butter = ¼ lb.

1 stick butter = ½ cup

1 stick butter = 8 Tbsp.

beans, 1 lb. dried = 2–2½ cups (depending on the size of the beans)

bell pepper, 1 large = 1 cup chopped

cheese, hard (for example, cheddar, Swiss, Monterey Jack, mozzarella), 1 lb. grated = 4 cups

cheese, cottage, 1 lb. = 2 cups

chocolate chips, 6-oz. pkg. = 1 scant cup

crackers (butter, saltines, snack), 20 single crackers = 1 cup crumbs

herbs, 1 Tbsp. fresh = 1 tsp. dried

lemon, 1 medium-sized = 2–3 Tbsp. juice

lemon, 1 medium-sized = 2–3 tsp. grated rind

mustard, 1 Tbsp. prepared = 1 tsp. dry or ground mustard

oatmeal, 1 lb. dry = about 5 cups dry

onion, 1 medium-sized = ½ cup chopped

Pasta

macaroni, penne, and other small or tubular shapes, 1 lb. dry = 4 cups uncooked

noodles, 1 lb. dry = 6 cups uncooked

spaghetti, linguine, fettucine, 1 lb. dry = 4 cups uncooked

potatoes, white, 1 lb. = 3 medium-sized potatoes = 2 cups mashed

Potatoes, sweet, 1 lb. = 3 medium-sized potatoes = 2 cups mashed

rice, 1 lb. dry = 2 cups uncooked

sugar, confectioners', 1 lb. = 3½ cups sifted

whipping cream, 1 cup unwhipped = 2 cups whipped

whipped topping, 8-oz. container = 3 cups

yeast, dry, 1 envelope (¼ oz.) = 1 Tbsp.

Recipe and Ingredient Index

A

Apple Breakfast Risotto, 25
apple juice
    Apple Breakfast Risotto, 25
    Polish Kraut and Apples, 213
apples
    Apple Breakfast Risotto, 25
    Breakfast Apple Cobbler, 27
    Honey-Orange Pork Roast, 158–159
    Korean-Inspired BBQ Shredded
      Pork, 177
    Polish Kraut and Apples, 213
    Polish Sausage and Sauerkraut, 215
    Pork Chops with Apples, 189
applesauce
    Brisket with Tomatoes and Sauerkraut, 113
apricot jam or preserves
    Beef Chuck Barbecue, 107
    Simple Savory Chicken, 41
Asian-Style Chicken with Pineapple, 61

B

bacon and bacon drippings
    Chicken Noodle Soup, 263
    Polish Sausage and Sauerkraut, 215
balsamic vinegar
    Garlic Mushroom Thighs, 41
    Herbed Pot Roast, 99
    Orange Garlic Chicken, 49
    Raspberry Balsamic Pork Chops, 195
Barbecue Chicken for Sandwiches, 57
Barbecued Brisket, 109
Barbecued Ham Steaks, 211
Barbecued Pulled Pork, 172–173
barbecue sauce
    Barbecue Chicken for Sandwiches, 57
    Barbecued Pulled Pork, 174–175
    Beef Chuck Barbecue, 107
    Boneless Barbecued Pork Ribs, 201
    Chuck Roast Beef Barbecue, 105
    Cranberry Chicken Barbecue, 51
    Easiest-Ever Country Ribs, 207

    Shredded BBQ Brisket, 111
    Stuffed Peppers, 139
BBQ Chicken Sandwiches, 55
BBQ Veggie Joes, 241
beans
    black
      Chili Chicken Stew with Rice, 275
      Mexican Rice and Beans, 229
      Quinoa and Black Beans, 231
      Salsa Ranch Chicken with Black Beans, 75
      Taco Chicken Bowls, 83
    cannellini
      Kielbasa Soup, 285
    garbanzo
      Chicken Chickpea Tortilla Soup, 271
      Italian Slow-Cooker Chicken, 73
      Vegetarian Coconut Curry, 233
      White Chile, 323
      White Chili, 323
    great northern
      Slow-Cooker Bean Soup, 293
      White Bean and Chicken Chili, 325
    kidney
      Chicken Chili, 319
      Jamaican Rice and Beans, 227
    measurements, 9
    navy
      The Best Bean and Ham Soup, 291
      Hearty Sausage and Beans, 219
      White Bean and Chicken Chili, 325
      White Chile, 323
    pinto
      Chipotle Chili, 321
      Hearty Sausage and Beans, 219
      White Chile, 323
    white
      Southwest Chicken and White Bean
       Soup, 273
beef
    brisket
      Barbecued Brisket, 109

Brisket with Tomatoes and Sauerkraut, 119
Shredded BBQ Brisket, 111
chuck roast
    Beef and Pepperoncini Hoagies, 125
    Beef Burgundy with Mushrooms, 115
    Beef Chuck Barbecue, 107
    Beef Roast with Homemade Ginger-
        Orange Sauce, 102–103
    Chuck Roast Beef Barbecue, 105
    Colorful Beef Stew, 279
    Easy Vegetable Beef Soup, 277
    Flavorful Pot Roast, 97
    Herbed Pot Roast, 99
    Hungarian Beef with Paprika, 117
    Italian Cheesesteak Sandwiches, 123
    Marinated Chuck Roast, 93
    Tostadas, 133
chuck steak
    No-Beans Chili, 327
cooking temperatures, 9
corned beef
    Guinness Corned Beef, 149
English roast
    Italian Beef Sandwiches, 127
flank steak
    Fabulous Fajitas, 129
    Four-Pepper Steak, 119
    Marinated Flank Steak with Broccoli, 121
Green Chile Roast, 101
ground
    Cheesy Beef and Pork Meatloaf, 144–145
    Chili in a Slow Cooker, 329
    Meatloaf, 141
    Meatloaf With Sweet Tomato Glaze,
        146–147
    Mexican Meatloaf, 143
    Stuffed Peppers, 139
Pot Roast, 95
round steak
    Fajita Steak, 131
    No-Beans Chili, 327
stew meat
    Beef Goulash, 137
Beef and Pepperoncini Hoagies, 125
Beef Burgundy with Mushrooms, 115

Beef Chuck Barbecue, 107
Beef Goulash, 137
Beef Roast with Homemade Ginger-Orange
    Sauce, 102–103
beer
    Polish Sausage and Sauerkraut, 215
bell pepper
    Beef Chuck Barbecue, 107
    Beef Goulash, 137
    Cheesy Beef and Pork Meatloaf, 144–145
    Chicken Chili, 319
    Chili in a Slow Cooker, 329
    Chops in the Crock, 191
    Colorful Beef Stew, 279
    Enchilada Soup, 313
    Fabulous Fajitas, 129
    Four-Pepper Steak, 119
    Fresh Veggie and Herb Omelet, 15
    Ham Omelet, 13
    Hungarian Beef with Paprika, 117
    Jambalaya, 89
    Jiffy Jambalaya, 221
    Lentils Swiss-Style, 237
    Memories of Tucson Chicken, 63
    Pork Thai Stew, 283
    Quinoa and Black Beans, 231
    Shrimp Jambalaya, 246–247
    Slow-Cooker Chicken Fajitas, 81
    Stuffed Peppers, 139
    Sweet-and-Sour Chicken, 59
    Sweet-and-Sour Ribs, 205
    Tostadas, 135
    White Chile, 323
black olives
    Savory Lentil Soup, 301
Boneless Barbecued Pork Ribs, 201
Bragg liquid aminos
    Asian-Style Chicken with Pineapple, 61
bread(s). see also garlic bread; rolls and buns
    Breakfast Casserole, 19
    French, for French Onion Soup, 307
bread crumbs
    Cheesy Beef and Pork Meatloaf, 144–145
    Meatloaf With Sweet Tomato Glaze, 146–147
Breakfast Apple Cobbler, 27
Breakfast Bake, 21

Breakfast Casserole, 19
Brisket with Tomatoes and Sauerkraut, 113
broccoli
    Broccoli Cheese Soup, 309
    Fresh Veggie and Herb Omelet, 15
    Marinated Flank Steak with Broccoli, 121
    Pork Chops With Asian Flair, 199
    Vegetarian Coconut Curry, 233
Broccoli Cheese Soup, 309
Brown-Sugar-and-Dijon Marinated Pork
    Roast, 163
Brown Sugar Pork Chops, 197
buns. *See* rolls and buns
burgundy
    Beef Burgundy with Mushrooms, 115
butternut squash
    Chipotle Chili, 321
    Creamy Butternut Squash Soup, 311
    Vegetarian Coconut Curry, 233

C
cabbage
    Guinness Corned Beef, 149
Cajun Catfish, 257
Cajun seasoning
    Jambalaya, 89
Carnitas, 185
carrots
    BBQ Veggie Joes, 241
    Beef Goulash, 137
    Chicken and Vegetable Soup, 265
    Chicken and Vegetable Soup with Rice, 267
    Creamy Butternut Squash Soup, 311
    Fresh Tomato Soup, 303
    Garlic Pork Roast, 153
    Guinness Corned Beef, 149
    Herbed Pot Roast, 99
    Lentil Spinach Soup, 299
    Magra's Chicken and Rice, 87
    No-Beans Chili, 327
    Pot Roast, 95
    Savory Lentil Soup, 301
    Shepherd Stew, 289
    Slow-Cooker Bean Soup, 293
    Split Pea Soup, 295
    Vegetable Soup Galore, 297

Vegetarian Coconut Curry, 233
    White Bean and Chicken Chili, 325
Catfish, Cajun, 257
cereal mix
    Breakfast Apple Cobbler, 27
cheddar cheese soup
    Broccoli Cheese Soup, 309
cheese
    Breakfast Bake, 21
    cheddar
        Breakfast Casserole, 19
        Cheesy Beef and Pork Meatloaf, 144–145
        Chicken Chickpea Tortilla Soup, 271
        Ham Omelet, 13
        Mexican Meatloaf, 143
        Mexican Rice and Beans, 229
    feta
        Fresh Veggie and Herb Omelet, 15
    Gruyère
        French Onion Soup, 307
    Lentils Swiss-Style, 237
    Mexican blend
        Chili Chicken Stew with Rice, 275
    mozzarella
        Breakfast Casserole, 19
        Easy Slow-Cooker Italian Chicken, 69
        Italian Beef Sandwiches, 127
        Italian Cheesesteak Sandwiches, 123
    Parmesan
        Italian Frittata, 17
    provolone
        Beef and Pepperoncini Hoagies, 125
        Italian Beef Sandwiches, 127
        Italian Cheesesteak Sandwiches, 123
    Taco Chicken Bowls, 83
    Velveeta
        Broccoli Cheese Soup, 309
Cheesy Beef and Pork Meatloaf, 144–145
chicken
    breast
        Asian-Style Chicken with Pineapple, 61
        Barbecue Chicken for Sandwiches, 57
        Chicken and Vegetable Soup with Rice, 267
        Chicken Chickpea Tortilla Soup, 271
        Chicken Chili, 319

Chicken Taco Salad, 85
Chili Chicken Stew with Rice, 275
Creamy Italian Chicken, 71
Easy Enchilada Shredded Chicken, 79
Easy Slow-Cooker Italian Chicken, 69
Italian Slow-Cooker Chicken, 73
Marinated Chicken Bits, 43
Orange Garlic Chicken, 49
Pineapple Chicken, 47
Quick Italian Chicken Strips with
    Veggies, 67
Salsa Ranch Chicken with Black Beans, 75
Slow-Cooker Chicken Fajitas, 81
Southwest Chicken and White Bean
    Soup, 273
Southwestern Shredded Chicken, 77
Tex-Mex Soup with Crunchy Tortillas, 269
Chicken and Vegetable Soup, 265
Chicken Noodle Soup, 263
cooking temperatures, 9
Cranberry Chicken Barbecue, 51
Jambalaya, 89
shredded
    White Chile, 323
Soy Honey Chicken, 33
thighs
    BBQ Chicken Sandwiches, 55
    Chicken Cacciatore with Vegetables, 65
    Chicken Dijon Dinner, 37
    Chipotle Chili, 321
    Cranberry Chili Chicken, 45
    Honey Garlic Chicken, 31
    Magra's Chicken and Rice, 87
    Simple Savory Chicken, 41
    Slow-Cooker Honey Mustard Chicken, 35
    Sweet-and-Sour Chicken, 59
    Taco Chicken Bowls, 83
    Zesty Barbecued Chicken, 53
White Bean and Chicken Chili, 325
Chicken and Vegetable Soup, 265
Chicken and Vegetable Soup with Rice, 267
Chicken Cacciatore with Vegetables, 65
Chicken Chickpea Tortilla Soup, 271
Chicken Chili, 319
Chicken Dijon Dinner, 37

Chicken Noodle Soup, 263
Chicken Taco Salad, 84
Chili Chicken Stew with Rice, 275
Chili in a Slow Cooker, 329
chili paste
    Pork Chops With Asian Flair, 199
chili sauce
    Cranberry Chili Chicken, 45
    Sweet-and-Sour Kielbasa, 217
Chipotle Chili, 321
Chops in the Crock, 191
Chuck Roast Beef Barbecue, 105
cilantro
    Quinoa and Black Beans, 231
    Salsa Lentils, 235
    Tasty Pork Tacos, 187
Coca-Cola
    Roast Pork Sauerkraut, 161
coconut curry sauce
    Vegetarian Coconut Curry, 233
coconut milk
    Jamaican Rice and Beans, 227
cod fillet
    Spiced Cod, 253
Colorful Beef Stew, 279
corn
    Chicken Noodle Soup, 263
    Chili Chicken Stew with Rice, 275
    Enchilada Soup, 313
    Memories of Tucson Chicken, 63
    Mexican Rice and Beans, 229
    Quinoa and Black Beans, 231
    Southwest Chicken and White Bean Soup,
        273
    Taco Chicken Bowls, 83
    Vegetable Soup Galore, 297
    White Chile, 323
Corned Beef, Guinness, 149
crabmeat
    Seafood Gumbo, 249
cranberries
    Honey-Orange Pork Roast, 158–159
Cranberry Chicken Barbecue, 51
Cranberry Chili Chicken, 45
Cranberry Pork Roast, 155
cranberry sauce

Cranberry Chicken Barbecue, 51
Cranberry Chili Chicken, 45
Cranberry Pork Roast, 155
cream cheese
    Creamy Italian Chicken, 71
cream of chicken soup
    Creamy Italian Chicken, 71
    Salsa Ranch Chicken with Black
      Beans, 75
cream of tomato soup
    Stuffed Peppers, 139
cream, when to add, 9
Creamy Butternut Squash Soup, 311
Creamy Italian Chicken, 71

D
Dijon mustard
    Beef Chuck Barbecue, 107
    Brown-Sugar-and-Dijon Marinated Pork
      Roast, 163
    Chicken Dijon Dinner, 37
    Lemon Dijon Fish, 251
    Raspberry Balsamic Pork Chops, 197
    Slow-Cooker Honey Mustard Chicken, 35
    Terrific Tenders, 170–171
Dr Pepper
    Barbecued Pulled Pork, 174–175
dry onion soup mix
    Meatloaf, 141
    Roast Pork Sauerkraut, 161

E
Easiest-Ever Country Ribs, 207
Easy Enchilada Shredded Chicken, 79
Easy Pork Loin, 167
Easy Slow-Cooker Italian Chicken, 69
Easy Vegetable Beef Soup, 277
edamame
    Soy Honey Chicken with, 33
eggs
    Breakfast Bake, 21
    Breakfast Casserole, 19
    Fresh Veggie and Herb Omelet, 15
    Ham Omelet, 13
    Italian Frittata, 17
enchilada sauce

Easy Enchilada Shredded Chicken, 79
Enchilada Soup, 313
Enchilada Soup, 313
evaporated milk
    Broccoli Cheese Soup, 309

F
fajitas
    Fabulous Fajitas, 129
    Slow-Cooker Chicken Fajitas, 81
Fajita Steak, 131
fish
    Cajun Catfish, 257
    Herbed Flounder, 255
    Lemon Dijon Fish, 251
    Spiced Cod, 253
Flavorful Pot Roast, 97
flounder fillets
    Herbed Flounder, 255
Four-Pepper Steak, 119
freezer bags, labeling, 4
freezer meals
    freezing tips, 4
    guide to, 2–3
French Onion Soup, 307
Fresh Tomato Soup, 303
Fresh Veggie and Herb Omelet, 15
frozen fruit
    Fruity Oatmeal, 23
frozen meat, cooking temperatures for, 9
frozen mixed vegetables
    Asian-Style Chicken with Pineapple, 61
    Easy Vegetable Beef Soup, 277
    Quick Kielbasa Soup, 287
    Vegetable Soup Galore, 297
Fruity Oatmeal, 23

G
garlic bread
    Marinated Chicken Bits served with, 43
    Quick Italian Chicken Strips with Veggies
      served with, 67
Garlic Mushroom Thighs, 41
Garlic Pork Roast, 153
ginger ale
    Barbecued Ham Steaks, 211

Greek yogurt
    Chicken Chickpea Tortilla Soup, 271
    Southwestern Shredded Chicken, 77
green beans
    Chicken and Vegetable Soup with Rice, 267
    Chicken Noodle Soup, 263
Green Chile Roast, 101
green chiles
    Chicken Chickpea Tortilla Soup, 271
    Green Chile Roast, 101
    Memories of Tucson Chicken, 63
    Southwestern Shredded Chicken, 77
    Tex-Mex Soup with Crunchy Tortillas, 269
green onions
    Chipotle Chili, 321
    Seafood Gumbo, 249
Guinness Corned Beef, 149
Gumbo, 315

H

ham
    Breakfast Bake, 21
    Ham Omelet, 13
    Shrimp Jambalaya, 246–247
ham bone
    The Best Bean and Ham Soup, 291
ham hocks/shanks
    Shepherd Stew, 289
    Slow-Cooker Bean Soup, 293
    Split Pea Soup, 295
Ham Omelet, 13
Ham Steaks, Barbecued, 211
hash brown potatoes
    Ham Omelet, 13
Hearty Sausage and Beans, 219
heavy cream
    Creamy Butternut Squash Soup, 311
    Tomato Basil Soup, 305
Herbed Flounder, 255
Herbed Pot Roast, 99
herbs (fresh), when to add, 9
honey
    Honey Garlic Chicken, 31
    Honey-Orange Pork Roast, 158–159
    Pot Roast, 95
    Saucy Spareribs, 203

    Slow-Cooker Honey Mustard Chicken, 35
    Soy Honey Chicken, 33
Honey Garlic Chicken, 31
Honey-Orange Pork Roast, 158–159
horseradish
    Guinness Corned Beef, 149
    Pot Roast, 95
hot sauce
    Fresh Veggie and Herb Omelet, 15
    Jambalaya, 89
    Korean-Inspired BBQ Shredded Pork, 177
    Spicy Pulled Pork Sandwiches, 179
Hungarian Beef with Paprika, 117

I

Italian Beef Sandwiches, 127
Italian Cheesesteak Sandwiches, 123
Italian dressing/dressing mix
    Barbecued Brisket, 109
    Flavorful Pot Roast, 97
    Italian Cheesesteak Sandwiches, 123
    Quick Italian Chicken Strips with Veggies, 67
Italian Frittata, 17
Italian Slow-Cooker Chicken, 73

J

jalapeño pepper
    Salsa Lentils, 235
    Shredded Pork Tortilla Soup, 281
    Tostadas, 133
Jamaican Rice and Beans, 227
Jambalaya, 89
    Jiffy Jambalaya, 221
    Shrimp Jambalaya, 246–247

K

ketchup
    Barbecued Ham Steaks, 211
    Barbecued Pulled Pork, 172–173
    BBQ Veggie Joes, 241
    Chops in the Crock, 191
    Chuck Roast Beef Barbecue, 105
    Country-Style Ribs, 209
    Korean-Inspired BBQ Shredded Pork, 177
    Meatloaf, 141
    Meatloaf With Sweet Tomato Glaze, 146–147

Mexican Meatloaf, 143
Pot Roast, 95
Saucy Spareribs, 203
Spicy Pulled Pork Sandwiches, 179
Sweet-and-Sour Chicken, 59
Sweet-and-Sour Ribs, 205
Kielbasa Soup, 285
Kielbasa Soup, Quick, 287
Kielbasa, Sweet-and-Sour, 217
Korean-Inspired BBQ Shredded Pork, 177

L

labeling freezer bags, 4
legumes. *See* beans; lentils
Lemon Dijon Fish, 251
Lemon Sweet Pork Chops, 193
lentils
    BBQ Veggie Joes, 241
    Lentil Spinach Soup, 299
    Lentils Swiss-Style, 237
    Lentil Tacos, 239
    Salsa Lentils, 235
    Savory Lentil Soup, 301
    Shepherd Stew, 289
Lentil Spinach Soup, 299
Lentils Swiss-Style, 237
Lentil Tacos, 239
lid, of slow cooker, 8
lima beans
    Vegetable Soup Galore, 297
liquid smoke
    Barbecued Brisket, 109
    Meatloaf, 141

M

Magra's Chicken and Rice, 87
manual slow cookers, 5–6
maple syrup
    Brown Sugar Pork Chops, 197
    Raspberry Balsamic Pork Chops, 197
Marinated Chicken Bits, 43
Marinated Flank Steak with Broccoli, 121
mashed potato flakes
    The Best Bean and Ham Soup, 291
measurements, cooked and dried bean, 9
Meatloaf, 141

Meatloaf With Sweet Tomato Glaze, 146–147
meat thermometer, 9
Memories of Tucson Chicken, 63
Mexican Meatloaf, 143
Mexican Rice and Beans, 229
molasses
    Spicy Pulled Pork Sandwiches, 179
Mrs. Dash Italian Medley Seasoning Blend
    Italian Slow-Cooker Chicken, 73
Mrs. Dash Original Seasoning Blend
    Slow-Cooker Bean Soup, 293
mushrooms
    Beef Burgundy with Mushrooms, 115
    Chicken and Vegetable Soup, 265
    Chicken Dijon Dinner, 37
    Garlic Mushroom Thighs, 41
    Ham Omelet, 13
    Italian Slow-Cooker Chicken, 73
    Simple Savory Chicken, 41
    Vegetarian Coconut Curry, 233
mustard. *see also* Dijon mustard
    BBQ Chicken Sandwiches, 55
    Chuck Roast Beef Barbecue, 105
    Slow-Cooker Honey Mustard Chicken, 35
    Zesty Barbecued Chicken, 53

N

No-Beans Chili, 327
noodles
    Chicken Noodle Soup, 263

O

oats
    Fruity Oatmeal, 23
    Meatloaf, 141
    Stuffed Peppers, 139
okra
    Gumbo, 315
    Jambalaya, 89
    Seafood Gumbo, 249
omelets
    Fresh Veggie and Herb Omelet, 15
    Ham Omelet, 13
Onion Soup, French, 307
onion soup mix. *See* dry onion soup mix
Orange Garlic Chicken, 49

orange juice
    Beef Roast with Homemade Ginger-Orange
      Sauce, 103
    Honey-Orange Pork Roast, 158–159
    Orange Garlic Chicken, 49
    Pork Chops With Asian Flair, 199
orange marmalade
    Cranberry Chili Chicken, 45
    Pork Chops With Asian Flair, 199
orange roughy fillets
    Lemon Dijon Fish, 251

P

Paprika, Hungarian Beef with, 117
pasta
    Creamy Italian Chicken, 71
    Easy Slow-Cooker Italian Chicken, 69
    Kielbasa Soup, 285
    Pork Chops With Asian Flair, 199
    Shrimp Marinara, 245
    when to add, 9
peanut butter
    Pork Thai Stew, 283
peas
    Chicken Noodle Soup, 263
    Vegetable Soup Galore, 297
pepperoncini peppers
    Beef and Pepperoncini Hoagies, 125
    Italian Beef Sandwiches, 127
pineapple and pineapple juice
    Asian-Style Chicken with Pineapple, 61
    Pineapple Chicken, 47
    Raspberry Balsamic Pork Chops, 197
    Sweet-and-Sour Chicken, 59
    Sweet-and-Sour Kielbasa, 217
    Sweet-and-Sour Ribs, 205
Pineapple Chicken, 47
Polish Kraut and Apples, 213
Polish Sausage and Sauerkraut, 215
pork. *see also* ham; sausage
    butt roast
      Barbecued Pulled Pork, 174–175
      Honey-Orange Pork Roast, 158–159
      Savory Pork Roast, 157
      Tasty Pork Tacos, 187
    cooking temperatures, 9

ground
    Cheesy Beef and Pork Meatloaf, 144–145
Ham Omelet, 13
Kielbasa Soup, 285
loin
    Easy Pork Loin, 167
    Salsa Verde Pork, 183
    Savory Pork Loin, 169
    Shredded Pork Tortilla Soup, 281
    Spicy Pulled Pork Sandwiches, 179
loin roast
    Brown-Sugar-and-Dijon Marinated Pork
      Roast, 163
    Cranberry Pork Roast, 153
    Garlic Pork Roast, 153
    Terrific Tenders, 170–171
Polish Sausage and Sauerkraut, 215
Quick Kielbasa Soup, 287
shoulder blade steaks
    Teriyaki Pork Steak with Sugar Snap
      Peas, 165
shoulder roast
    Barbecued Pulled Pork, 172–173
    Carnitas, 185
    Sweet Mustard Pulled Pork, 181
sirloin tip roast
    Korean-Inspired BBQ Shredded Pork, 177
Sweet-and-Sour Kielbasa, 217
tenderloin
    Pork Thai Stew, 283
pork chops
    Chops in the Crock, 191
    Lemon Sweet Pork Chops, 193
    Pork Chops with Apples, 189
    Pork Chops With Asian Flair, 199
    Raspberry Balsamic Pork Chops, 195, 197
pork ribs
    Boneless Barbecued Pork Ribs, 201
    Country-Style Ribs, 209
    Easiest-Ever Country Ribs, 207
    Saucy Spareribs, 203
    Sweet-and-Sour Ribs, 205
Pork Thai Stew, 283
potatoes
    Chicken Cacciatore with Vegetables, 67

Garlic Pork Roast, 153
Herbed Pot Roast, 99
Pot Roast, 95
Quick Kielbasa Soup, 287
Slow-Cooker Bean Soup, 293
Vegetable Soup Galore, 297
Pot Roast, 95
Prego sauces
Easy Slow-Cooker Italian Chicken, 69
programmable slow cookers, 5–6
prosciutto
Italian Frittata, 17
Pulled Pork, Barbecued, 172–173
Pulled Pork Sandwiches, Spicy, 179
Pulled Pork, Sweet Mustard, 181
Pulled Pork With Dr. Pepper, 174–175

Q

QR code, 2
Quick Italian Chicken Strips with Veggies, 67
Quick Kielbasa Soup, 287
quick-read meat thermometer, 9
quinoa
Enchilada Soup, 313
Quinoa and Black Beans, 231

R

ranch dressing mix
Flavorful Pot Roast, 97
Salsa Ranch Chicken with Black Beans, 75
Raspberry Balsamic Pork Chops, 195
red bell pepper
Chicken Cacciatore with Vegetables, 67
Fresh Veggie and Herb Omelet, 15
Ribs
Easiest-Ever Country Ribs, 207
Sweet-and-Sour Ribs, 205
rice
Arborio, in Apple Breakfast Risotto, 25
Chicken and Vegetable Soup with Rice, 267
Chili Chicken Stew with Rice, 275
Chops in the Crock with, 191
Honey Garlic Chicken with, 31
Jamaican Rice and Beans, 227
Jambalaya, 89
Jiffy Jambalaya, 221

Magra's Chicken and Rice with, 87
Marinated Flank Steak with Broccoli with, 121
Mexican Rice and Beans, 229
Pineapple Chicken served with, 47
Pork Thai Stew, 283
Shrimp Jambalaya, 246–247
Soy Honey Chicken with, 33
Stuffed Peppers, 139
Sweet-and-Sour Chicken with, 59
Taco Chicken Bowls, 83
Roast Pork Sauerkraut, 161
rolls and buns
Barbecue Chicken for Sandwiches, 57
Barbecued Pulled Pork, 172–173
BBQ Chicken Sandwiches, 55
BBQ Veggie Joes, 241
Beef and Pepperoncini Hoagies, 125
Beef Chuck Barbecue, 107
Chuck Roast Beef Barbecue, 105
Italian Beef Sandwiches, 127
Italian Cheesesteak Sandwiches, 123
Pulled Pork with Dr Pepper, 174–175
Savory Pork Loin, 169
Shredded BBQ Brisket, 111
Spicy Pulled Pork Sandwiches, 179

S

salsa
Fajita Steak, 131
Lentil Tacos, 239
Mexican Meatloaf, 143
Mexican Rice and Beans, 229
Salsa Lentils, 235
Salsa Ranch Chicken with Black Beans, 75
Salsa Verde Pork, 183
Southwest Chicken and White Bean Soup,
273
Taco Chicken Bowls, 83
Tostadas, 135
Salsa Lentils, 235
Salsa Ranch Chicken with Black Beans, 75
Salsa Verde Pork, 183
saltine crackers
Mexican Meatloaf, 143
sandwich rolls. *See* rolls and buns
Saucy Spareribs, 203

sauerkraut
    Brisket with Tomatoes and Sauerkraut, 113
    Hearty Sausage and Beans, 219
    Polish Kraut and Apples, 213
    Polish Sausage and Sauerkraut, 215
    Roast Pork Sauerkraut, 161
sausage
    Breakfast Casserole, 19
    Gumbo, 315
    Hearty Sausage and Beans, 219
    Jambalaya, 89
    Jiffy Jambalaya, 221
    Polish Kraut and Apples, 213
    Polish Sausage and Sauerkraut, 215
Savory Lentil Soup, 301
Savory Pork Loin, 169
Savory Pork Roast, 157
Seafood Gumbo, 249
7-Up
    Barbecued Ham Steaks, 211
Shepherd Stew, 289
sherry
    Lentils Swiss-Style, 237
Shredded BBQ Brisket, 111
Shredded Pork, Korean-Inspired, 177
Shredded Pork Tortilla Soup, 281
shrimp
    Gumbo, 315
    Jambalaya, 89
    Seafood Gumbo, 249
    Shrimp Jambalaya, 246–247
    Shrimp Marinara, 245
Shrimp Jambalaya, 246–247
Shrimp Marinara, 245
Simple Savory Chicken, 39
Slow-Cooker Bean Soup, 293
Slow-Cooker Chicken Fajitas, 81
Slow-Cooker Honey Mustard Chicken, 35
slow cookers
    choosing, 4
    getting to know your, 6
    having more than one, 5
    "hot spot" in, 6
    manual vs. programmable, 5–6
    size of, 4–5
slow cooking

meat temperatures, 9
    tips and tricks, 8–9
snow peas
    Pork Chops With Asian Flair, 199
soups
    The Best Bean and Ham Soup, 291
    Broccoli Cheese Soup, 309
    Chicken and Vegetable Soup with Rice, 267
    Chicken Chickpea Tortilla Soup, 271
    Chicken Noodle Soup, 263
    Creamy Butternut Squash Soup, 311
    Easy Vegetable Beef Soup, 277
    Enchilada Soup, 313
    French Onion Soup, 307
    Fresh Tomato Soup, 303
    Gumbo, 315
    Kielbasa Soup, 285
    Lentil Spinach Soup, 299
    Quick Kielbasa Soup, 287
    Savory Lentil Soup, 301
    Shredded Pork Tortilla Soup, 281
    Slow-Cooker Bean Soup, 293
    Southwest Chicken and White Bean Soup, 273
    Split Pea Soup, 295
    Tex-Mex Soup with Crunchy Tortillas, 269
    Tomato Basil Soup, 305
    Vegetable Soup Galore, 297
sour cream, when to add, 9
Southwest Chicken and White Bean Soup, 273
Southwestern Shredded Chicken, 77
Soy Honey Chicken, 33
soy sauce
    Beef Roast with Homemade Ginger-Orange Sauce, 102–103
    Brown-Sugar-and-Dijon Marinated Pork Roast, 163
    Chicken Dijon Dinner, 37
    Easy Pork Loin, 167
    Honey Garlic Chicken, 31
    Korean-Inspired BBQ Shredded Pork, 177
    Marinated Chicken Bits, 43
    Marinated Chuck Roast, 93
    Marinated Flank Steak with Broccoli, 119
    Pineapple Chicken, 47
    Pork Chops With Asian Flair, 199

Saucy Spareribs, 203
Savory Pork Loin, 169
Soy Honey Chicken, 33
Sweet-and-Sour Chicken, 59
Sweet Mustard Pulled Pork, 181
Zesty Barbecued Chicken, 53
spaghetti squash
    Simple Savory Chicken with, 41
Spareribs, Saucy, 203
Spiced Cod, 253
Spicy Pulled Pork Sandwiches, 179
spinach
    Italian Slow-Cooker Chicken, 73
    Kielbasa Soup, 285
    Lentil Spinach Soup, 299
Split Pea Soup, 295
Sprite
    Barbecued Ham Steaks, 211
squash. *see also* butternut squash
    Chicken and Vegetable Soup, 265
    Simple Savory Chicken with spaghetti, 41
sriracha sauce
    Chuck Roast Beef Barbecue, 105
    Saucy Spareribs, 203
steak sauce
    Pot Roast, 95
stewed tomatoes
    Brisket with Tomatoes and Sauerkraut, 113
    Chops in the Crock, 191
    Lentils Swiss-Style, 237
    No-Beans Chili, 327
stews
    Chili Chicken Stew with Rice, 275
    Colorful Beef Stew, 279
    Pork Thai Stew, 283
    Shepherd Stew, 289
Stuffed Peppers, 139
sugar snap peas
    Teriyaki Pork Steak with Sugar Snap Peas,
        165
Sweet-and-Sour Chicken, 59
Sweet-and-Sour Kielbasa, 217
Sweet-and-Sour Ribs, 205
Sweet Mustard Pulled Pork, 181
sweet potatoes
    Creamy Butternut Squash Soup, 311

Honey-Orange Pork Roast, 158–159

T
Taco Chicken Bowls, 83
taco seasoning
    Chicken Taco Salad, 85
    Mexican Meatloaf, 143
    Salsa Lentils, 235
    Salsa Ranch Chicken with Black Beans, 75
    Slow-Cooker Chicken Fajitas, 81
    Tostadas, 135
Tasty Pork Tacos, 187
temperature for cooking meat, 9
Teriyaki Pork Steak with Sugar Snap Peas, 165
teriyaki sauce
    Pork Thai Stew, 283
    Teriyaki Pork Steak with Sugar Snap Peas,
        165
Terrific Tenders, 170–171
Tex-Mex Soup with Crunchy Tortillas, 269
thawing freezer meals, 3
The Best Bean and Ham Soup, 291
Tomato Basil Soup, 305
tomatoes (canned)
    Chicken Cacciatore with Vegetables, 65
    Chicken Chili, 319
    Chicken Taco Salad, 85
    Chili Chicken Stew with Rice, 275
    Chili in a Slow Cooker, 329
    Easy Enchilada Shredded Chicken, 79
    Easy Vegetable Beef Soup, 277
    Enchilada Soup, 313
    Fajita Steak, 131
    Four-Pepper Steak, 119
    Gumbo, 315
    Jambalaya, 89
    Jiffy Jambalaya, 221
    Lentil Spinach Soup, 299
    Seafood Gumbo, 249
    Shrimp Jambalaya, 246–247
    Shrimp Marinara, 245
    Slow-Cooker Chicken Fajitas, 81
    Southwestern Shredded Chicken, 77
    Tomato Basil Soup, 305
    White Bean and Chicken Chili, 325
tomatoes (fresh)

Chicken Chickpea Tortilla Soup, 271
Fresh Tomato Soup, 303
Fresh Veggie and Herb Omelet, 15
Memories of Tucson Chicken, 63
Salsa Verde Pork, 183
Shredded Pork Tortilla Soup, 281
Tex-Mex Soup with Crunchy Tortillas, 269
Vegetable Soup Galore, 297
tomato juice
Meatloaf With Sweet Tomato Glaze, 146–147
Mexican Rice and Beans, 229
Savory Pork Loin, 169
tomato paste
Beef Burgundy with Mushrooms, 115
Chipotle Chili, 321
Colorful Beef Stew, 279
Fresh Tomato Soup, 303
Gumbo, 315
Pot Roast, 95
Quick Kielbasa Soup, 287
Savory Lentil Soup, 301
Shrimp Marinara, 245
Sweet-and-Sour Ribs, 205
White Bean and Chicken Chili, 325
tomato sauce
Cheesy Beef and Pork Meatloaf, 144–145
Fajita Steak, 131
No-Beans Chili, 327
Savory Lentil Soup, 301
Sweet-and-Sour Ribs, 205
tomato soup
Easy Vegetable Beef Soup, 277
Fresh Tomato Soup, 303
Stuffed Peppers, 139
tortilla chips
Chicken Chickpea Tortilla Soup, 271
tortillas
Carnitas, 185
Fabulous Fajitas, 129
Fajita Steak, 131
Tasty Pork Tacos, 187
Tex-Mex Soup with Crunchy Tortillas, 269
Tostadas, 132–133
Tostadas, 132–133
turkey, cooking temperatures for, 9

V
V8 juice
Chili in a Slow Cooker, 329
vegetables. *see also* frozen mixed vegetables;
    individual types of vegetables
    kept on bottom of slow cooker, 8
    using precut, 3
Vegetable Soup Galore, 297
Vegetarian Coconut Curry, 233

W
White Bean and Chicken Chili, 325
White Chile, 323
white wine
    French Onion Soup, 307
    Salsa Verde Pork, 183
Worcestershire sauce
    Barbecued Brisket, 1090
    Barbecued Pulled Pork, 172–173
    BBQ Veggie Joes, 241
    Beef Goulash, 137
    Chops in the Crock, 191
    Chuck Roast Beef Barbecue, 105
    Country-Style Ribs, 209
    Fabulous Fajitas, 129
    Green Chile Roast, 101
    Lemon Dijon Fish, 251
    Savory Pork Loin, 169
    Spicy Pulled Pork Sandwiches, 179
    Stuffed Peppers, 139
    Sweet-and-Sour Ribs, 205
    Zesty Barbecued Chicken, 53

Z
Zesty Barbecued Chicken, 53
zucchini
    Memories of Tucson Chicken, 63

About the Author

Hope Comerford is a mom, wife, elementary music teacher, blogger, recipe developer, public speaker, ALM Zone fit leader, Young Living Essential Oils essential oil enthusiast/educator, and published author. In 2013, she was diagnosed with a severe gluten intolerance and since then has spent many hours creating easy, practical, and delicious gluten-free recipes that can be enjoyed by both those who are affected by gluten and those who are not.

Growing up, Hope spent many hours in the kitchen with her Meme (grandmother) and her love for cooking grew from there. While working on her master's degree when her daughter was young, Hope turned to her slow cookers for some salvation and sanity. It was from there she began truly experimenting with recipes and quickly learned she had the ability to get a little more creative in the kitchen and develop her own recipes.

In 2010, Hope started her blog, *A Busy Mom's Slow Cooker Adventures*, to simply share the recipes she was making with her family and friends. She never imagined people all over the world would begin visiting her page and sharing her recipes with others as well. In 2013, Hope self-published her first cookbook, *Slow Cooker Recipes 10 Ingredients or Less and Gluten-Free*, and then later wrote *The Gluten-Free Slow Cooker*.

Hope became the new brand ambassador and author of Fix-It and Forget-It in mid-2016. Since then, she has brought her excitement and creativeness to the Fix-It and Forget-It brand. Through Fix-It and Forget-It, she has written *Fix-It and Forget-It Lazy & Slow*, *Fix-It and Forget-It Healthy Slow Cooker Cookbook*, *Fix-It and Forget-It Favorite Slow Cooker Recipes for Mom*, *Fix-It and Forget-It Favorite Slow Cooker Recipes for Dad*, *Fix-It and Enjoy-It Welcome Home Cookbook*, *Fix-It and Forget-It Holiday Favorites*, *Fix-It and Forget-It Cooking for Two*, *Fix-It and Forget-It Crowd Pleasers for the American Summer*, *Fix-It and Forget-It Dump Dinners and Dump Desserts*, *Fix-It and Forget-It Welcome Home Diabetic Cookbook*, *Fix-It and Forget-It Welcome Home Harvest Cookbook*, and *Fix-It and Forget-It Instant Pot Cookbook*.

Hope lives in the city of Clinton Township, Michigan, near Metro Detroit. She's a native of Michigan and still lives there. She has been happily married to her husband and best friend, Justin, since 2008. Together they have two children, Ella and Gavin, who are her motivation, inspiration, and heart. In her spare time, Hope enjoys traveling, singing, cooking, reading books, spending time with friends and family, and relaxing.

FIX-IT and FORGET-IT®